LOUISE MURDOCK'S LIVING LEGACY:
A HISTORY OF THE WICHITA ART MUSEUM

ISBN 0-939324-44-X
Cover: *Kansas Cornfield* (1933), John Steuart Curry, oil on canvas

The spirit of volunteerism has always been strong at the Wichita Art Museum. Louise Caldwell Murdock set the tone in 1915 when she left her city the means to acquire the works of art that became the heart of the museum. Mrs. Murdock has many descendants in spirit who have given unselfishly of their time to see her dream carried out.

Like much of what has happened at the Wichita Art Museum in its 56 years, this book represents the efforts of dedicated volunteers. What started as a project for the museum's 50th anniversary stretched to fill several years of borrowed afternoons spent researching and writing. The volunteers who produced this book deserve many thanks for their time and their perseverance in seeing this project to completion.

The book they have produced is not an academician's history, but a human interest documentation of the people and personalities who have shaped the Wichita Art Museum. It gives us a special appreciation for the role that volunteers have played and for the unique public-private partnership that makes our museum work.

J. Richard Gruber, Director
The Wichita Art Museum
October 1991

When Betty Minkler agreed to plan and manage a year-long series of celebrations for the Wichita Art Museum's approaching 50th anniversary in 1985, she strongly felt that this event should also signal the writing of the museum's yet-unrecorded history.

Betty wanted Anna Lee Drake and Sarah (Sue) Amsden, both known for their journalistic leanings and for their participation in the original volunteer efforts at the museum, to undertake the challenge of writing the narrative. Jean Clark, who assisted them, was adept at creative writing and historical research.

They were joined by two other volunteers: Bertha Milbank, a former president of the Wichita Art Museum Members, who was a valuable researcher, and Alta Brock, who was pursuing graduate work in editorial studies.

The group, which became known as "The Book Committee," worked well together despite delays, disruptions and more discouragements than could be foreseen. As the work stretched from months to years, they maintained their interest in the task and its purpose. ❧

Louise Caldwell Murdock and Elizabeth Stubblefield Navas were central in shaping the Wichita Art Museum. The articles reproduced here are helpful in understanding their roles and their personalities.

SOME RECOLLECTIONS OF LOUISE CALDWELL MURDOCK

by Bess Innes Galland
(From a talk given at the meeting of Wichita Art Museum Members Inc., September 17, 1962)

It was 46 years ago that Wichita received a golden gift from one of her wisest and most generous citizens. The gift was the Roland P. Murdock Collection of American Art and the donor was Louise Caldwell Murdock. She was an extraordinary person, remarkable in any community at any time, but more so for having lived her entire life in a small Kansas town just emerging from frontier days.

While her family was not among those early settlers who came here in a covered wagon, she was nonetheless of pioneer stock as her father, J. Edwards Caldwell, brought his wife and three small daughters to Wichita from New York State in the early eighties. He established a china and crockery store on North Main Street, a business that prospered as long as it was in existence.

Louise attended public school, but her schooling ended when she was not more than fourteen, as she was needed at home to help care for an invalid sister. The youngest of the three Caldwell daughters, Mary, went to Baker University and upon graduation married Samuel McRoberts who eventually became president of the National City Bank of New York.

Louise loved music, and possessing an excellent alto voice became a member of the choir of the First Methodist Church. Also in the choir were two other charming young women: Emma Hills, who became the mother of Harriet Stanley, and Emma Smith, the mother of the Imboden girls. The male voices were those of W.E. Stanley, Hiram Imboden, and Roland P. Murdock. This happy association led to the marriage of Emma Hills to W.E. Stanley, the marriage of the other Emma to Hiram Imboden, and Louise Caldwell became the wife of Roland Murdock. With the marriage of a fourth couple, the popularity of the choir can well be imagined.

Roland Murdock's service to his church did not end when his term as chorister was ended. He initiated the custom of standing at the entrance every Sunday morning to welcome each member of the congregation with a warm handclasp and friendly smile. To be greeted by this tall, distinguished-looking gentleman was an accepted feature of going to church.

I know the relationship of the Murdocks is bewildering to anyone who has not grown up with them.

At the top of the family tree we find Thomas, a man of Scotch-Irish descent, an itinerant Methodist preacher. He fathered three sons, Marshall Mortimer (Col. Marsh), the first owner of *The Wichita Eagle,* whose wife was Victoria Mayberry; Roland Pierpont, business manager of *The Eagle,* who married Louise Caldwell; and Benton of El Dorado.

My memory of Louise Murdock goes back to my childhood. I remember her getting out of the phaeton in front of our house, tying the horse, and with her handsome, obstreperous little boy by the hand, coming to call on my mother. Those were pre-first-name days and she was Mrs. Murdock to me then and even to her intimate friends, and she was so known throughout her life.

From the beginning of their marriage the Roland Murdocks took an active part in the social life of the day which was somewhat formal but delightful, for "Society" was made up of people from the East, from Illinois, Ohio and Indiana, who had had much the same background of refinement and means. The hospitality of the Murdock home was enjoyed not only by their circle of friends but by out-of-town notables. Visiting bishops always stayed there. Jane Addams was a visitor, as was Fanny Farmer, Arthur Capper, and the heads of the Chautauqua Institute.

Mrs. Murdock was enthusiastic about the Chautauqua movement, as it was called, which provided means of self-help through courses of home study. Along with this was the week-long regional session when nationally known speakers were brought for lectures and top ranking musicians performed. These were held in smaller communities where the year-round monotony was otherwise unbroken by cultural stimulus. Mrs. Murdock was featured year after year as a speaker on art.

It may surprise you to hear that Mrs. Murdock's pet hobby was cooking, which she looked upon as an art and essential to gracious living. She took pleasure in preparing meals for her family. As always, eager for the best for her community, she brought Fanny Farmer here to conduct a cooking school, and then Mrs. Ewing, whose classes were attended by practically every housewife in town, even those who barely knew the inside of their own kitchens.

In accompanying her husband on his frequent business trips to New York she was able to see the originals of paintings and sculpture which she had heretofore known only by reproductions. The great collections, such as the Frick and the Havemeyer were forming. Having the privilege of seeing this art caused her to be aware of the narrow horizons of the women of her own community and the lack of climate for any creative effort. So the idea of the 20th Century Club was conceived and became a reality with its founding in January 1899. Mrs. Murdock was its first president, serving from 1899 to 1906.

At the time of its organization, Twentieth Century had a scant handful of members. The present yearbook lists a total of 1,577: 900 senior members, 116 in the Evening 20th Century, 200 in the Cornelias (the young married group), and 367 in the Junior or High School classification. It is staggering to think of the number of women who have in the 63 years of the club's history broadened their horizons through the classes, programs and various other activities it has provided.

As is usual with residential areas in growing cities, the neighborhood surrounding the Murdock home on North Topeka began to deteriorate. A new house, designed by Mrs. Murdock, was built on the corner of Park Place and 15th Street. A smaller one for her parents was built on the same lot.

It was not long after moving into the new house that Mr. Murdock died. The only living son was a constant source of worry to his mother. From his earliest years he had managed to elude education. After a try at Wichita's public schools, he was enrolled in the Military Academy at Bordentown, New Jersey, from which he returned with little more than an eye-catching uniform. Having parents who loved music and being endowed with a remarkable tenor voice, he was given every musical advantage. Young Roll, who never had an angelic thought in his life, had a voice right out of the heavenly choir. And what an opportunity for a present-day psychiatrist! Had there been one to turn his talent into a career, his story might have been very different. As it was, he was seldom at home, preferring the pleasure spots of large cities where his escapades were spectacular and costly.

Now that there were no longer home ties, Mrs. Murdock went to New York to study interior design with Frank Alvah Parsons, the founder of the Parsons School of Fine and Applied Art. Subsequently she returned to Wichita and opened a studio on the top floor of the Caldwell-Murdock Building which she and her father had built, and became the first interior decorator in Kansas. Scarcely were the announcements out, when she received a letter from a young woman just graduated from high school in another Kansas town, saying that she wished to become an interior decorator and asking for an interview. The young woman was Elizabeth Stubblefield (later Mrs. Rafael

Navas), who became assistant to Mrs. Murdock. As they worked together, a deep bond of respect, affection and understanding developed between the older and the younger woman, to whom ultimately was given the responsibility of purchasing art works for the Roland P. Murdock Collection.

In the first months of the interior decorating venture, clients were largely friends of Mrs. Murdock who came to her for help in their furnishing problems. It was soon demonstrated that she had an unerring sense of quality and an innate sense of style. She placed in the home of a Wichita banker the first large Persian rug, or carpet, ever seen here. David Walker and Hazel Brooks are among those who inherited and still enjoy finely designed furniture selected by Mrs. Murdock. Larger commissions for public buildings were not long in coming, such as the Wichita Club, the remodeled Crawford Theatre, the Wichita Country Club and the new Carnegie Library.

The library was a burning issue at that time, just as it is today. Andrew Carnegie had emerged from his steel mills with the offer to pay the initial cost of a brand new $100,000 library. This is the story, published in the *Ladies Home Journal* for March 1916. It bears the title, "When a Wichita Woman Said 'I Will' ":

> . . .It was Mrs. Roland P. Murdock who realized that here was a chance for Wichita to outdo itself. Thereupon she set about coordinating all the talent the city possessed and set it working. For years, as an interior decorator and as an active club woman, she had done all that lay within her power to improve the artistic aspect of public buildings and to help the housewives in her own and neighboring states toward an artistic betterment of their homes.

> All the furniture in the library is from models secured by her, as are the lighting fixtures and the other equipment. In addition she arranged with Mr. Arthur E.Covey, ex-Kansan and associate of Messrs. Frank Brangwyn and Jules Guerin, to paint the three murals shown here, and with Miss Elizabeth Stubblefield of Wichita, to create the sunflower windows symbolic of the state. At the time of Mrs. Murdock's death. . . it was learned she had left her entire fortune to the securing of pictures by American artists for Wichita.

Three weeks after the dedication of the library, Mrs. Murdock died. She was the victim of cancer for which, in the earlier stages of the disease, she had undergone two operations. If that were not enough, she was left with X-ray burns which often caused her great distress and discomfort. She survived a third operation by only a few days. When her will was examined, it was learned that upon the death of her son, sister and mother, her property was to be put into a trust fund and the interest accruing was to be used for the buying of an art collection for the City of Wichita.

It was 22 years before the art fund became available, during which time Mrs. Navas with her co-trustee handled the business of the estate and looked after the welfare of Mrs. Murdock's survivors.

With Mrs. Murdock much in my thoughts the past week, I have asked some of her young friends what they remember about her. One said she remembered her lovely smile. Another recalled her clear blue eyes with their steady gaze. Another remembered her as a tall woman, statuesque, with an air of elegance about her. I know to most of you she is a legendary figure, but it is my hope that in recalling her life to you, she has come alive for a few moments and given you the assurance that she was a real person, very vital, very human. ❧

ELIZABETH NAVAS

A Tribute by Howard E. Wooden, former director of the Wichita Art Museum
(As printed in The Art Gallery *magazine, September 1979)*

Most of you are aware that Elizabeth Stubblefield Navas died in New York City on Friday morning March 30 at the age of 92. It just so happened that I was in New York at the time and learned of her death late that afternoon. Her memorial service was held in Wichita but because of an airline strike, I was unable regretfully to return home in time to attend. Generally, whenever I spent more than a day in New York, I had luncheon with Mrs. Navas, and I had planned on having her join me at luncheon on Monday.

Luncheon with Elizabeth Navas was always a delightful affair. Her conversations were lively and informative for she spoke with the authority of first-hand experience. Each conversation was like a personal but unwritten chapter in American art history. She possessed a fabulous wealth of information – inside glimpses – on the American art scene that few people ever knew. I suspect I learned more about happenings in the 20th century world of American art by listening to Mrs. Navas than from any other single source.

Indeed, as an art museum director I consider it one of my greatest privileges to have known Mrs. Navas. She was the individual responsible for the development of the Roland P. Murdock Collection, one of the finest collections of American art in this country. She was a proud and determined woman; had she not been so, Wichita today would not be the possessor of this enviable collection. She had a keen mind and a keen eye, she was alert and perceptive and she possessed incredible foresight and superb taste . . . and much personal dignity. She knew intimately the art world, for over the years she had become closely acquainted with many artists, critics, collectors, museum directors and art gallery dealers. As she purchased works for the Murdock collection, she made few, if any, misjudgments. Indeed, her record of achievement is essentially unmatched. She was proud of the new museum here, and happy to know that the collection which she developed would be cared for. She was a native Kansan and truly cared, and she was trustful that the museum, its collections and its programs would be appreciated and fully supported.

What was so especially significant about Elizabeth Navas was her great courage. She never feared the unknown art. She returned to her alma mater, Columbia University, and became based in New York to broaden her training through courses there, and later at Harvard and Yale. She also studied at the great museums in New York and nearby.

She was married in 1917 to Rafael Navas, an accomplished concert pianist whose early training was in his native Spain and who later became a graduate of the Paris Conservatory. After her husband's death in 1939, Elizabeth Stubblefield Navas gradually achieved wide recognition for her abilities in assessing artworks. She served two terms as a trustee of the prestigious American Federation of Art and in 1967 was made honorary trustee, the first woman to receive this distinction.

In Wichita, others aware of the Mrs. Murdock's bequest were thinking about their own part of the responsibilities ahead. Would the community be ready to commit itself to building a museum for an art collection yet to be assembled? How many townspeople were even interested in art or art ownership? The year was 1920 and these were challenging questions for Walter Vincent, C.A. Seward, and others who agreed that a first step must be the organization of a group willing to start things moving. Their efforts established the Wichita Art Association. Its goals were to encourage the arts and to provide an art museum that would be able to receive and care for Mrs. Murdock's gift. The first board members were President Walter Vincent, Mrs. Henry J. Allen, Mrs. David Basham, Walter Crandall, Charles Englehart, Ed L. Davison, Mrs. Richard Gray, Charles H. Hatton, Mrs. E.E. Holmes, Mrs. Will K. Jones, Floris Nagelvoort, C.A. Seward, and Alton Smith. Within a year the new association had brought in works of noted artists for free exhibitions, established prizes for public school art students, and begun acquiring an art collection of its own. A regular schedule of public art classes soon followed. But when it came to finding fund-

ing for a museum building, the group promptly found itself facing a formidable problem.

Prospects remained discouraging until it was found that money for such a public building could be obtained through a bond

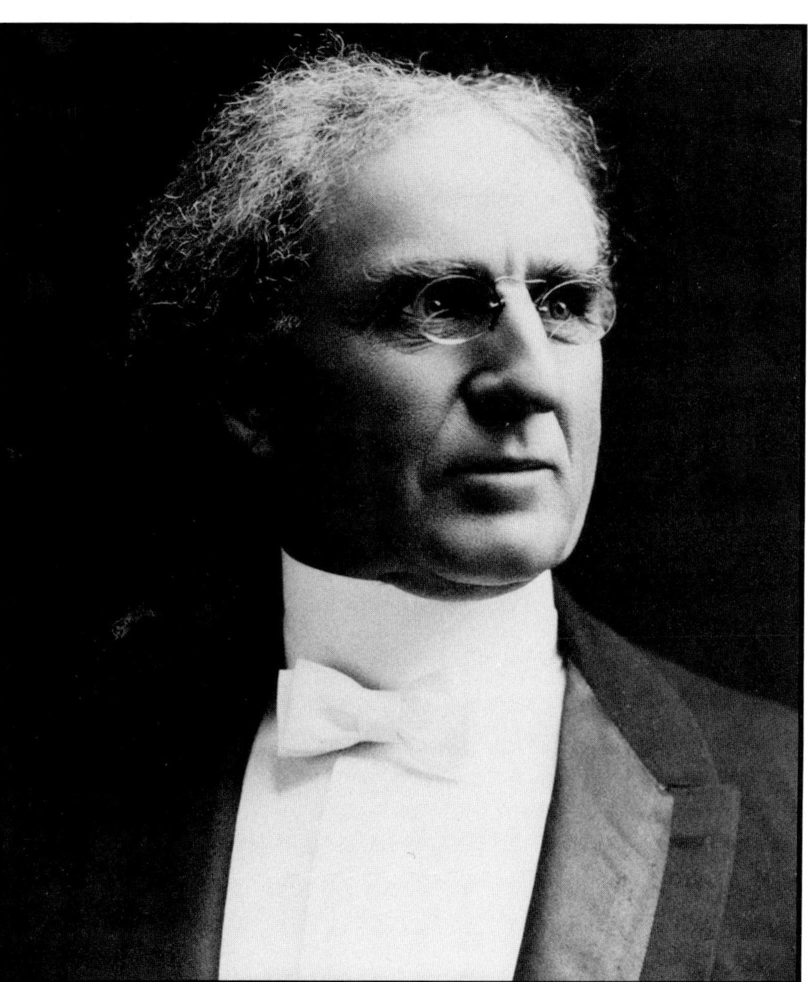

Louise Caldwell Murdock's husband, Roland Pierpoint Murdock, shown here in about 1905, was business manager of The Wichita Eagle. Photo courtesy of Wichita-Sedgwick County Historical Museum

issue by the Board of Park Commissioners. At this point the Park Board, which answered to the City Commission, assumed full managerial control of the evolving art museum. This arrangement was maintained for most of the next 30 years with two brief exceptions: a lease to the Wichita Art Association in 1935 and a lease to the University of Wichita's art department in 1951.

In addition to endorsing funding requests for the museum, the Board of Park Commissioners also provided further

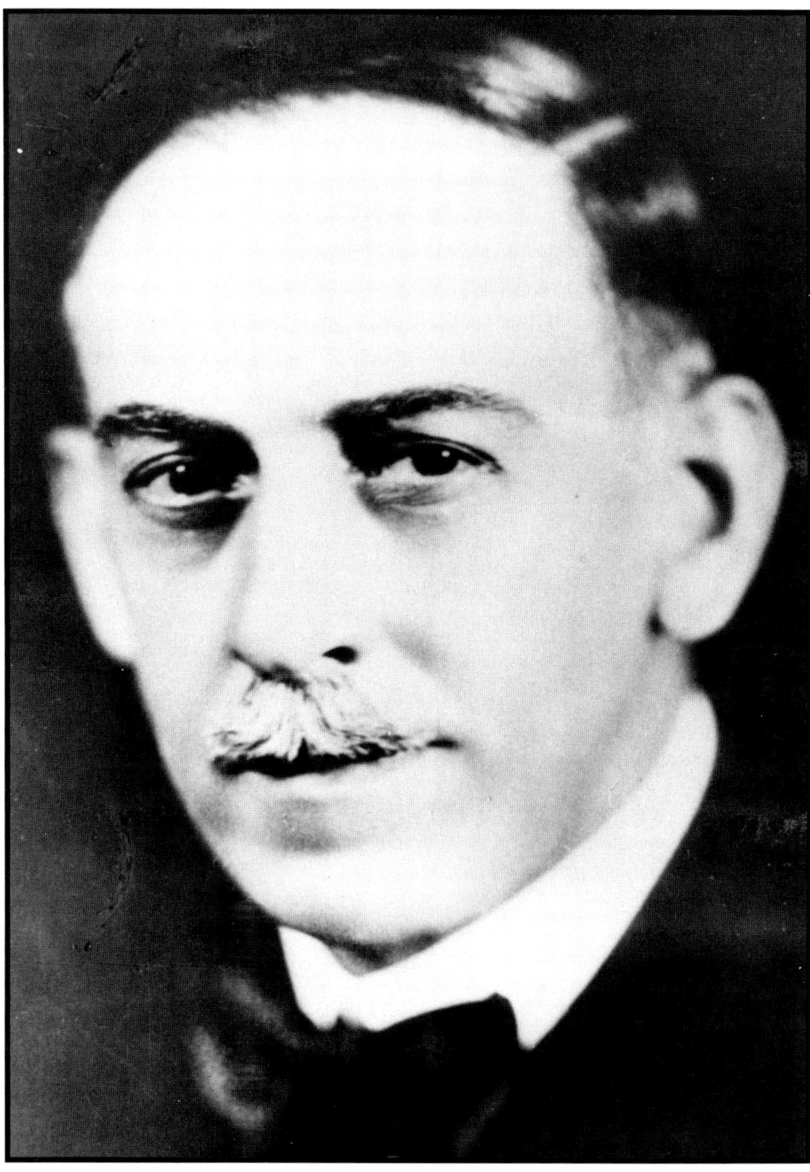

valuable assistance. One of the commissioners, L.W. Clapp, who was knowledgeable about architecture, traveled at his own expense to investigate modern museums. He recommended Clarence Stein, a highly regarded New York architect, to design the Wichita museum.[2] The commissioners concurred, Mr. Stein accepted, and on June 17, 1925, *The Wichita Eagle* followed with a forceful admonition to the public to "Build First Unit of Art Museum in Immediate Future:"

Immediate steps will be taken by the Wichita Art Association to secure for the city the first unit of an art museum to be built in a convenient location in one of the parks. A resolution to this effect was passed Tuesday evening at the regular monthly meeting of the association's Board of Directors at the Wichita city library.

The resolution concurred with that passed within the last month at the request of the civic committee by the Board of Directors of the Wichita Chamber of Commerce. It recommends that the first unit of the new building be included in the city's plans for immediate park improvements.

The erection of this building would satisfy that provision of the will of the late Mrs. R.P. Murdock which leaves the income from the Caldwell-Murdock building, 111 East Douglas Avenue, as a trust fund to be used at the death of the present beneficiaries, 'to purchase paintings and other objects of art for a permanent collection for Wichita, provided that at that time the city possesses a building suitable to house the collection.'

'Unless Wichita gets busy and has a building ready to house such a collection,' Walter Vincent said, 'we shall before very many years suddenly find ourselves losing this wonderful chance for the beginnings of a fine collection. And not only the beginnings will be lost, but also an ever-increasing fund, for as the years make the Caldwell-Murdock building more and more valuable, the income from this property will rise far above the $20,000 a year which it is now adding to the trust fund.'

The proposition which the building committee of the Art Association will put before the city park department is that this first unit of the museum be promptly built as a matter of park improvement. This first section would cost about $75,000 according to Mr. Vincent.

The city park department, under the state laws, is allowed to issue bonds for park improvements up to the amount of $1,500,000 outstanding at one time. 'At present,' Mr. Vincent said, 'the Wichita department has about $650,000 of bonds outstanding. If this

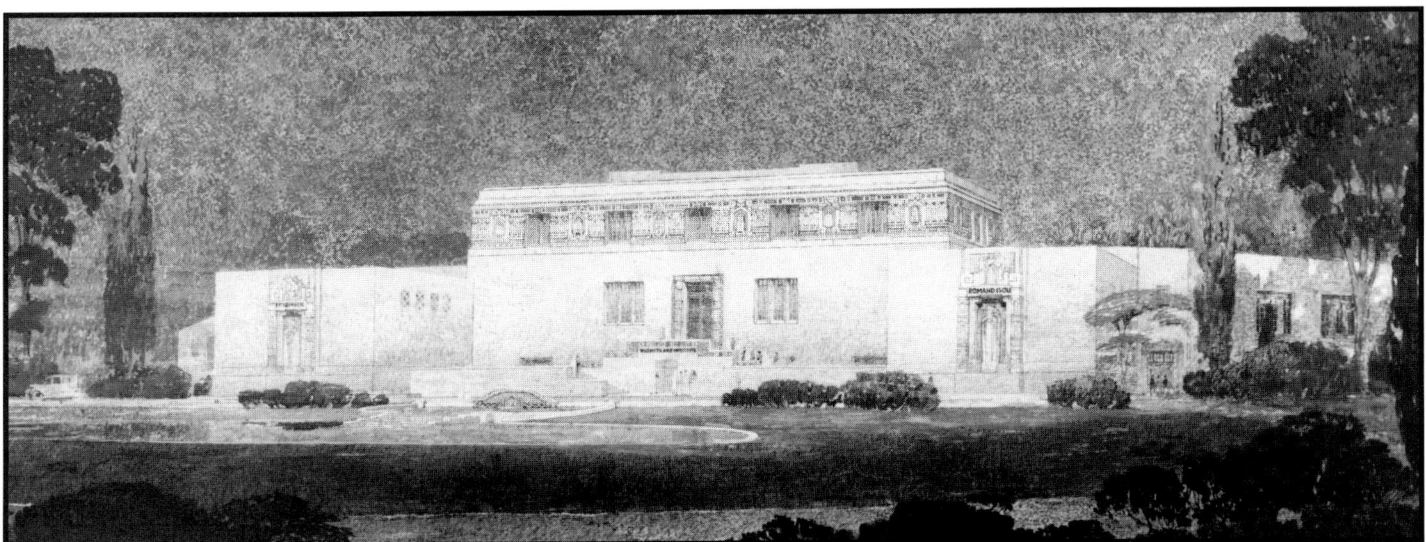

$75,000 is not used for this sort of park improvement, it will be used for some other, and we will run a great chance in the meantime of losing a wonderful art collection.

'The building should be of real beauty, an architectural asset to the city,' Mr. Vincent said. 'It should be as well a structure which we can enlarge as our collections grow. This is but the beginning, and it is the chance of a beginning that we must not let slip by through our failure to provide in time a suitable building in which to house a permanent art collection.'

The Art Association appointed a committee of L.W. Clapp, L.R. Hurd, W.C. Coleman, Alton Smith, C.M. Jackson, C.A. Seward, and Walter Vincent "to carry on with the work concerning the proposed building."

Things were moving at last. The president of the Park Board was authorized to purchase property for the museum. *Wichita This Week* advised the public in its September 12-18 issue of 1926 that "with the transfer last week, by sale and gift of approximately 7.65 acres of land in the West Riverside district, the city acquired a site for a municipal art museum." The spacious tract was a fortunate choice with a scenic outlook, facing a curve in the Little Arkansas River where it flows by Riverside Park. Here again Mr. Clapp earned his city's thanks. The article in *Wichita This Week* said that "L.W. Clapp. . . is chiefly responsible for the transaction through his

friendship with the Stackman family." The Stackmans were pioneer owners of the tract.

Wichita's five city commissioners, Mayor Frank Nighswonger, Ben Copley, C.C. Dehner, Frank Dunn, and A.J. Coombs, voted unanimously to build the museum and a $75,000 bond issue was floated on July 6, 1925. The project, however, was beset by a series of delays well into the 1930s. The Park Board's attention was drawn to other responsibilities, particularly the construction of a municipal airport. Meanwhile, adjustments to the museum blueprints were made in an effort to reduce the cost. The building's two wings were eliminated, leaving only its boxlike center. As changes in the plans were required, the architect's fees increased.

In July 1934 the Park Board appointed Godfrey Hartwell construction supervisor and sent him to New York City to confer with the architect. His compensation was $25 a day plus traveling expenses and a subsistence allowance. Work was soon under way with employees of the Works Progress Administration digging the footings for the wingless central unit of the Wichita Art Museum. The external decorative features of the original plans were left unchanged. They embodied symbols of Mayan and Pueblo Indian culture. The two-story structure was finished in earth-tone cast concrete. It had a large, double-doored second floor entrance flanked by a grand staircase in stone. &

New York architect Clarence Stein designed the museum to house the Murdock Collection.

Chapter Two
1935-1958

Dedication ceremonies for the Art Museum building began at 3 p.m. on Sunday, September 22, 1935. A brief concert by the American Legion Band was followed by Rabbi Harry Richmond's invocation. Walter Vincent, president of the Park Board, presented the museum to the citizens of Wichita. After Mayor Frank Nighswonger had accepted for the city, he presented the building in trust to the Wichita Art Association and gave the keys to its president, Maude Schollenberger.

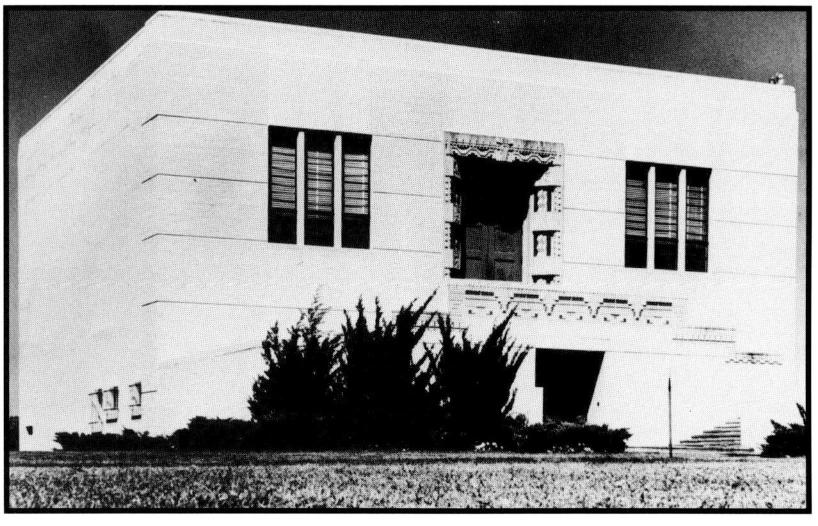

Without the wings architect Clarence Stein had designed, the central unit of the museum completed in 1935 was a small boxlike structure.

Doors were open to visitors until 9 in the evening and again during daylight hours throughout the following week. Visitors found an outstanding exhibition of art works, all on loan from museums and individual collectors. There were two paintings by Mary Cassatt, two Peter Bruegels, a Camille Corot, a Paul Cezanne, an Edward Hopper, a Gilbert Stuart, an Albert Ryder, and a Winslow Homer, among others. Wichitans were elated to have the paintings of these and other artists in their museum's first exhibition. The quality and scope of the exhibition undoubtedly contributed to the success of the opening, which was described in the October 1935 issue of *The Art Digest* as having had "an attendance count of more than 10,000 persons during its first week and 3,000 during the second." Wichita in 1935 had a population of just over 100,000.

The Art Digest congratulated Wichita upon the opening of its museum and quoted the principal speaker, Victor Murdock, editor of *The Wichita Eagle*, who said that

" . . . through generations to come, many thousands will visit the galleries of this edifice which we now open. Some will come in devotion to beauty. Some will come to seek the secret of skill in masterpieces. But most will come on humankind's eternal quest, searching for truth, instinctively feeling that art can reveal truth."

Among the members of the Wichita Art Association who presided in the galleries during the opening were R.T. Aitchison, Mrs. Winn Holmes, E. Walter Stipple, and Mrs. Ed. L. Davison.

The structure so long awaited was actually a building of only 11,750 square feet. It looked like a square box on an empty prairie. Architect Stein's original design envisioned a three-story central unit flanked by two-story wings, which would have considerably increased the floor space and greatly enhanced the overall effect. But the economics of the 1930s were stringent and the wings had to wait.

Even so, more than the construction of a building had been achieved by 1935. In the years since its founding in 1920, the Wichita Art Association had flourished in its own development as a teaching organization dedicated to studio art training and practice. It had the support of its own staff and trustees. The city recognized the Art Association as a civic asset and arranged for it to lease the new museum building. The lease continued from September 1935 to December 1942.

In 1937, the death of Cornelia S. Caldwell, the last of the three heirs named in Mrs. Murdock's will, activated the second directive of the Roland P. Murdock trust, allowing Mrs. Navas to begin acquiring an art collection for the City of Wichita. Her first selection, *Kansas Cornfield,* painted in

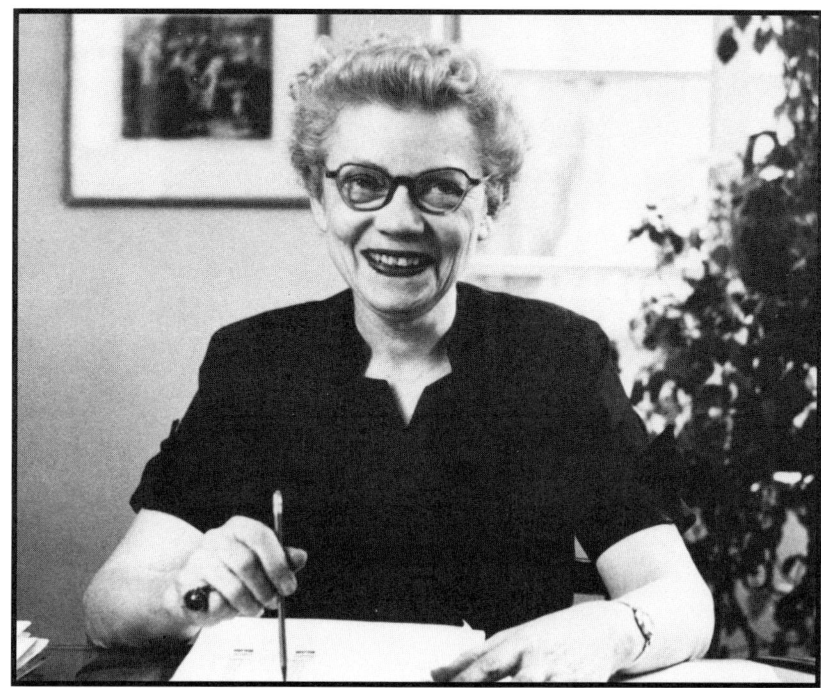

1933 by John Steuart Curry, was hung on June 7, 1939. In April 1940, the Murdock attorneys notified the city that the estate would be ready in early October to present 15 additional paintings. On November 8, Mrs. Navas came from New York to supervise the display of these works and to deliver a lecture about them in the museum auditorium.[3]

The acquisition of these first paintings caused profound changes at the little building on the river. Wichita Art Association members felt inconvenienced by the crowding, though the community at large was scarcely aware of the strains created when the small building came to house two art operations – the Art Association with its own collection and its burgeoning school, and the expanding Murdock Collection. By the end of 1942, the Art Association decided to buy the former L.R. Hurd residence at Third and Belmont in east Wichita, returning the vacated museum building to Park Board management.

The move resulted in long-standing confusion over the names and purposes of the Wichita Art Association and the Wichita Art Museum. The separation ended the strains of overcrowding but not citizen puzzlement about whether there were one or two organizations, and which was which. Many felt that one was enough to cover all art interests in a city the size of Wichita. From time to time, there were statements and proposals to this effect. In 1959 joint meetings were held by the two boards at the Lassen Hotel and at the Art Association "to evaluate needs." Nothing came of the efforts. In 1962 another serious effort at unification took place and it seemed well timed. The Art Museum was ready to add the long-foregone wings and the Art Association had plans for a fundraising drive to build a bigger facility. Representatives of each organization met four times during October "to identify obstacles and resolve differences." Their differences went unresolved, however, and the attempt collapsed.

The two organizations have remained separate – the Art Association (now called the Wichita Center for the Arts) as a privately-funded teaching center for the arts with a permanent art collection and galleries, and the city-owned Art Museum, with both public and private support. Each has flourished independently.

The 1942 departure of the Art Association left room for the growing Murdock Collection, but the museum had no organizational structure of its own. There was neither a board of directors nor a salaried director for operations. The city turned the museum over to the Park Board and its director, Alfred MacDonald. There it remained for the next eight years.

In New York, Mrs. Navas, ever uneasy about the welfare of the paintings assembled in Wichita, apparently concluded that a part-time unpaid director would be better than no museum director at all if this person could be her knowledgeable friend, Elizabeth "Bess" Innes Galland. Mrs. Galland

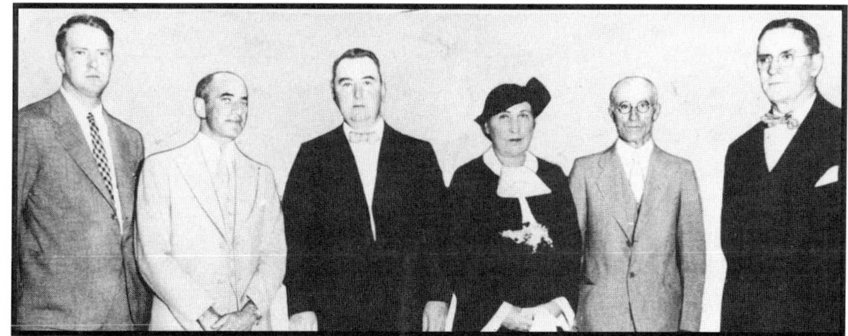

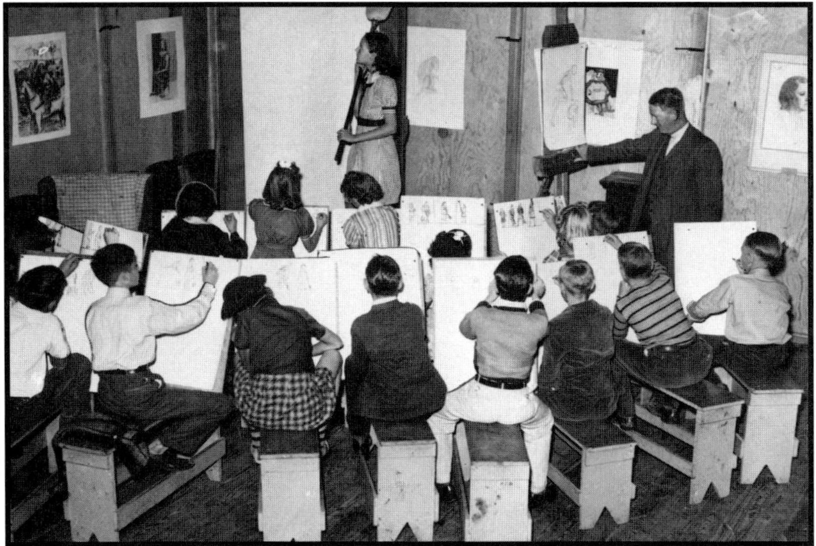

Harry Corbin and Dr. Eugene McFarland, chairman of the arts department, agreed to revive and expand the Advisory Council, which had been disbanded. The goal was a 25-member council that would draw wider community interest and support.

Mrs. Navas was not pleased to have the museum combined with another institution and it was difficult for those involved to agree on planning. Dr. McFarland finally went to New York hoping to reach an accord with Mrs. Navas regarding urgent problems and new procedures. A member of his staff recalled that he returned deeply discouraged. In August 1955 the university notified the City Commission that it would not seek a contract renewal for operation of the art museum once the current contract expired in 1956. When Dr. McFarland died in an automobile accident in the fall of 1955, the university requested a release from its contract "as soon as possible."

It became apparent to the Wichita City Commission that it must finally give the museum status as a department of the city with a board of its own. Mayor Claude de Vorss appointed two commissioners, A.E. Howse and H.D. Lester, to bring a report of the museum's history and an evaluation of its problems and prospects, plus their recommendations for action, to the next weekly commission meeting on November 1, 1955.

The report was thorough and extensive, recommending a seven-member board of directors for the museum. The commissioners then appointed Sam Bloomfield, president; W.J. Van Wormer, vice president; Harold Curry; Elizabeth "Bess" Innes Galland; Lee Phillips, Jr.; Mrs. Charles Rombold; Dr. John Shellito; and, as an alternate member, Robert J. Schaefer.

At its November 15 meeting, the City Commission filed City Ordinance #21-440 establishing the new board.These actions launched the museum into a new era of organizational stability, having a board of directors, statutory authority, and a budget of $15,000 for the coming year. The city also

served in a volunteer custodial capacity, interpreted by Mrs. Navas as "acting director," during the first three years of Park Board management, 1943 to 1946. She and others promoted an advisory council. Although the council idea was not endorsed at first by Alfred MacDonald, in 1945 it became a reality unopposed at Park Board headquarters. The first members of the council, which had no legal authority, were Mrs. David Basham, Mrs. Sheldon Coleman, the Reverend Jesse Clyde Fisher, Mrs. Galland, Mrs. Charles G. Higginson, Mrs. Charles Jackson, Mrs. Claude Lambe, Dr. L.W. Mayberry, M.C. Naftzger, Leo St. Clair, Mrs. W.A. Stippich, and Mrs. Ralph Varner.

During this period another important art collection arrived at the Wichita Art Museum, a gift from the Naftzger family. The first installation came to the museum in 1943 as a group of original American and European prints and drawings dating from the 16th through the 20th centuries. Included were several drawings and sculptures by the noted Yugoslavian artist Ivan Mestrovic (1883-1962). Eight years later, 61 prints were added to this L.S. and Ida L. Naftzger Collection, which was given to the Wichita Art Museum as a memorial from their children.

In December 1951 the Wichita City Commission ratified a resolution to have administration of the museum transferred to the University of Wichita in a five-year renewable contract. University President petitioned the District Court to grant it assured title and full control of the Murdock Collection. This assurance was granted in 1957.

Vice President Van Wormer presided at the first board meeting because President Bloomfield was out of town.[4] Alternate Robert Schaefer had replaced Lee Phillips, who apparently felt it inappropriate to serve since he was already a board member of the Wichita Art Association. Mr. Schaefer was elected the board's first secretary and Harold Curry became its first elected treasurer.

By October 1956 the museum had a professional director, Carroll Edward Hogan, a native of Iowa City, Iowa. He came to Wichita from Buffalo, New York, where he had served the Albright Art Gallery as assistant director and curator. He remained at the Wichita museum for nearly two years. Records of these first years, if any were kept, are unavailable. It has been recalled that Mr. Hogan complained that the museum and its valuable collection were getting short shrift from the city, and that Mr. Hogan was obliged to supply the building's first vacuum cleaner and stapler.

In 1956 Mrs. Navas's co-trustee of the Murdock Estate, John Parkinson, died. He was not replaced until 1957 when Judge E.E. Sattgast named Congressman Garner Shriver as co-trustee.

In New York, Mrs. Navas was always concerned about whether the paintings she was collecting were being cared for properly. During the interval when she was the sole trustee, she went to District Court for authorization to use trust funds to hire a conservator to inspect the artworks periodically and an accountant to make audits. She also asked for authority to spend $10,000 to publish a catalogue of the Murdock Collection, which she felt was important to the integrity of the collection. At the same time, she asked for $2,500 for her work on the catalog, and for an increase in the trustee's annual fee from $1,800 to $3,600. "It was my idea, asking for additional compensation," Eugene G. Coombs, the Wichita attorney who represented her, recalled in 1991. He felt

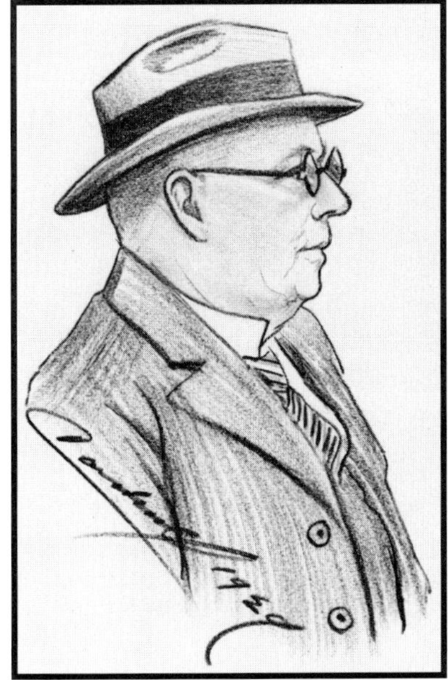

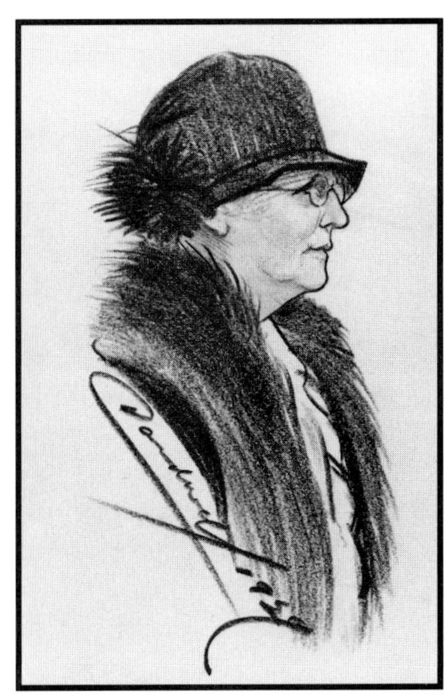

Mrs. Navas deserved greater compensation for doing the work to which she devoted much of her time. "She wouldn't ask for money," he said. Her true concern was the care of the collection.

The city challenged her on whether some of these expenditures fell within the terms of Mrs. Murdock's will, which called only for "the buying of an art collection for the City of Wichita." The District Court ruled in Mrs. Navas' favor, authorizing money for hiring a conservator, publishing a catalog, and compensating Mrs. Navas for her work on the catalogue, saying that these things were integral to the collection. The city appealed to the Supreme Court of Kansas, which sided with the lower court and Mrs. Navas. ❧

An important collection of American and European prints, drawings, and sculptures came to the museum from the Naftzger family as a memorial to L.S. and Ida L. Naftzger, shown here in drawings made in 1929.

Carroll Edward Hogan became the museum's first full-time director in 1956.

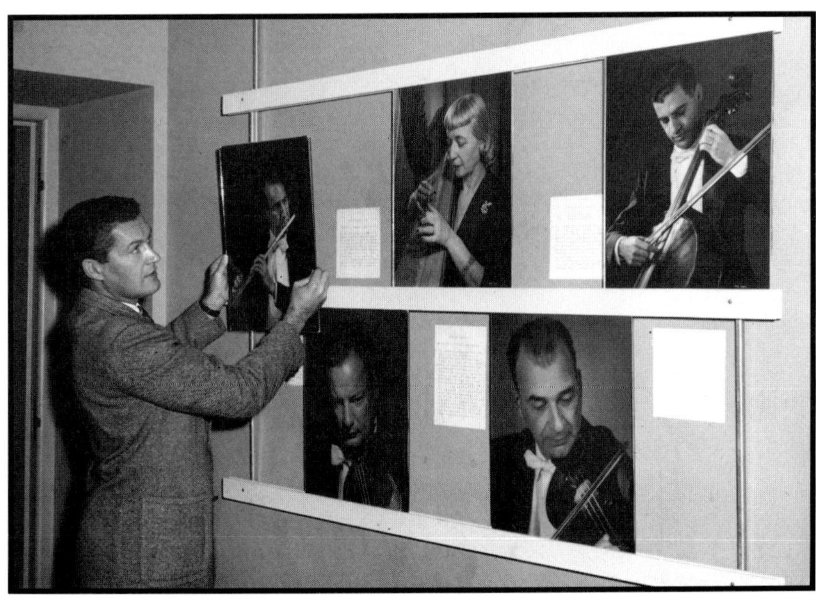

Chapter Three
1958-1961

Richard Grove was employed in 1958 as the museum's second director. He had a bachelor's degree in Latin American studies and a master's degree in art history from Mexico City College. Before coming to Wichita he was on the curatorial staff of the Taylor Museum, which belonged to the Fine Arts Center of Colorado Springs, Colorado. He served the Wichita Art Museum for six years. His profound dismay at its physical condition spurred him to work hard for its improvement. In a good-humored article published in *Wichita This Week,* he called

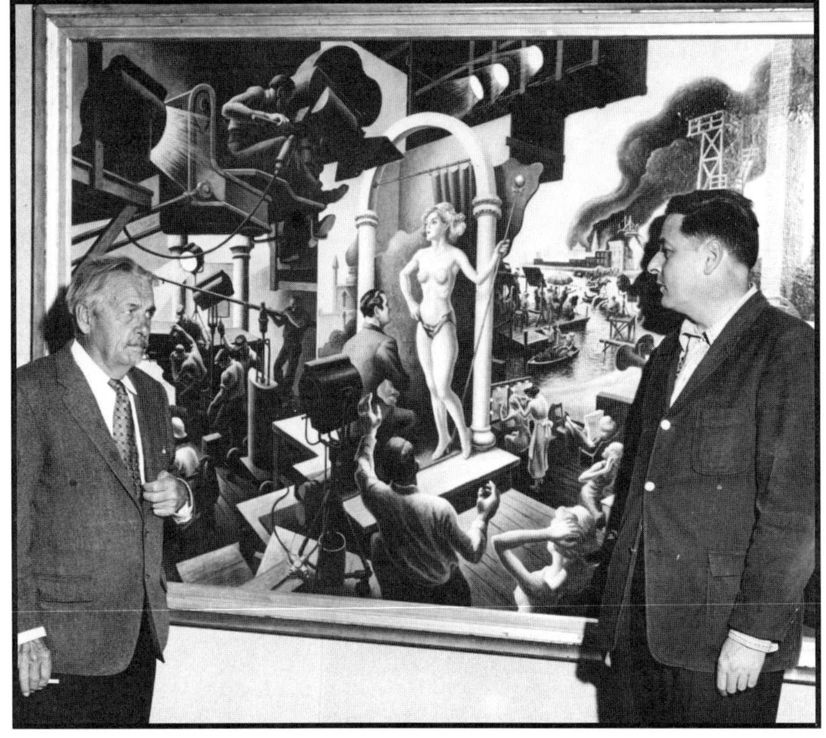

Richard Grove, right, shown with painter Thomas Hart Benton, served as director of the museum from 1958 until 1964.

attention to critically needed repairs, describing "the rippling lake formed in the museum's main gallery when it rained." Mr. Grove noted the periodic quagmire of the unpaved driveway and referred to opening day of an important exhibition:

> ...with five cars down to their axles in the mud and everyone very well dressed. You should have seen those people after they dug their cars out.... Termites marched in another time and munched the bottom off the front door. On sunny August days, famous paintings sagged and cracked in the fierce heat. Last summer I had to put a dozen of the most valuable 650 feet underground in the Hutchinson salt mines. Some cities have a conscience though, I know Wichita does. Recently they did the following:
> (1) they paved the driveway
> (2) waterproofed the building
> (3) (Later) installed a modern air-conditioning system
> (4) built a 700 square foot air-conditioned vault to house the collection.
> Meanwhile we all went to work. We painted the interior walls and filled the cracks. We panelled right over the dirt and fingerprints in three galleries. We shipped baled masterpieces off to expert restorers. Carried away by enthusiasm we even painted the front doors orange red to symbolize a brave new era.

By the spring of 1960, Emory Cox, director of parks, had contracted for the waterproofing of the leaking north and south exterior walls. That summer *The Wichita Eagle and Beacon* described the temporary removal of the best of the museum's paintings to the salt mines at Hutchinson and also commented: "Even more effective in the correction of heat and humidity problems was a good hot candlelit dinner provided for the Commissioners at the Museum on a torrid July night. Not long thereafter, the Commission reached one of its then-rare unanimous decisions: to air condition the Museum and to construct an improved storage vault for the collections."

After having become an autonomous entity under municipal government in 1955, the Wichita Art Museum evolved with a rapidity heartening to its faithful backers. One of these, Gwendolyn Naftzger, offered the museum's board of directors an idea that was promptly ap-

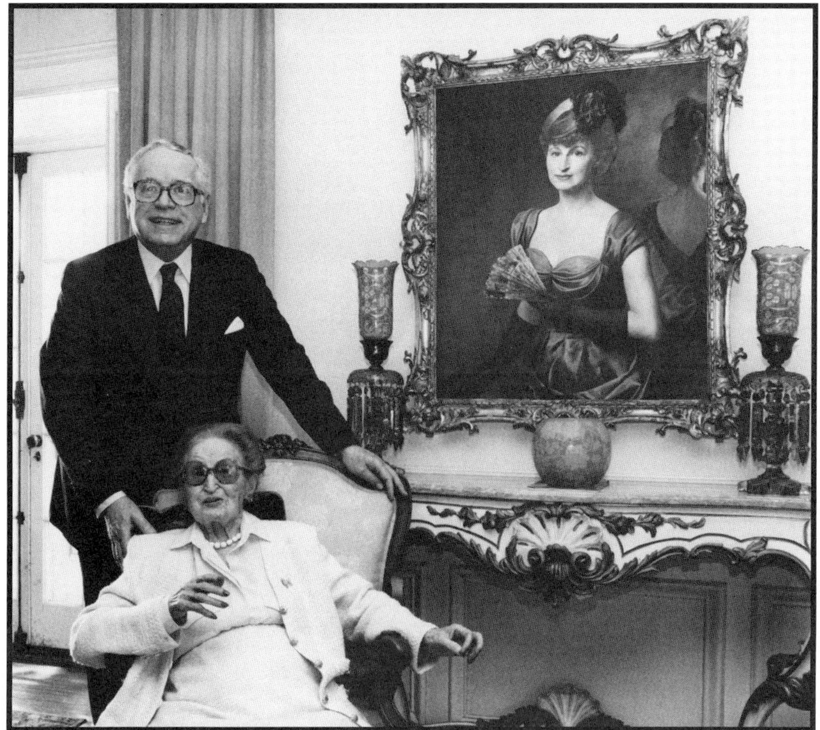

proved and destined to be valuable. In the years of the Advisory Council, she and other volunteers had carried buckets of Kool-Aid to the museum's inadequate kitchen when refreshments were expected. They were concerned, as well, about other improvements and repairs. Mrs. Naftzger was certain that a support group of women volunteers could benefit the museum.

The museum's city-appointed board approved the addition of a "members" organization. On November 2, 1959, a group of women recognized as potential leaders was invited to meet at the museum to propose a slate of officers. Mrs. Glenn Milburn of the museum board of directors presided as chairman pro-tem. The group was to be called The Wichita Art Museum Members with the acronym WAMM. The proposed officers were: Mrs. William Murfin, president; Mrs. Max Staley, vice president; Mrs. Willard Garvey, secretary; Mrs. Ralph Drake, treasurer; and Mrs. Glenn Milburn, adviser. The slate was accepted at the next meeting on November 23 and the new president soon named committees. They were working on bylaws and project plans before the year ended.

"NEW LIFE at ART MUSEUM" was the headline of the evening *Eagle's* lead editorial on February 6, 1960. It hailed:

> . . .a significant event in the cultural life of Wichita which took place Thursday night as the new Wichita Art Museum Members, Inc. held its first public lecture meeting. Despite bad weather more than 100 persons attended, most pulled there by the heartening evidence that at long last someone was doing something to encourage support for the Museum . . . what has happened is that a group of civic-minded women decided to quit talking about the sad state of affairs at the Museum in Riverside and do something about it. Sparked by

Gwendolyn Naftzger, these women decided to set up a program . . . to create interest in the Museum and lead people to join. In this way they hope to elicit the support, both in attendance and financially, so greatly needed . . . . We may be in the midst of an awakening in Wichita to our own rich cultural possibilities if wide public support can be enlisted. The auspicious start by The Wichita Art Museum Members, Inc. reinforces this effort and deserves public support."

Betty Murfin, WAMM President, presided over the organization's public debut that stormy night in February and asked

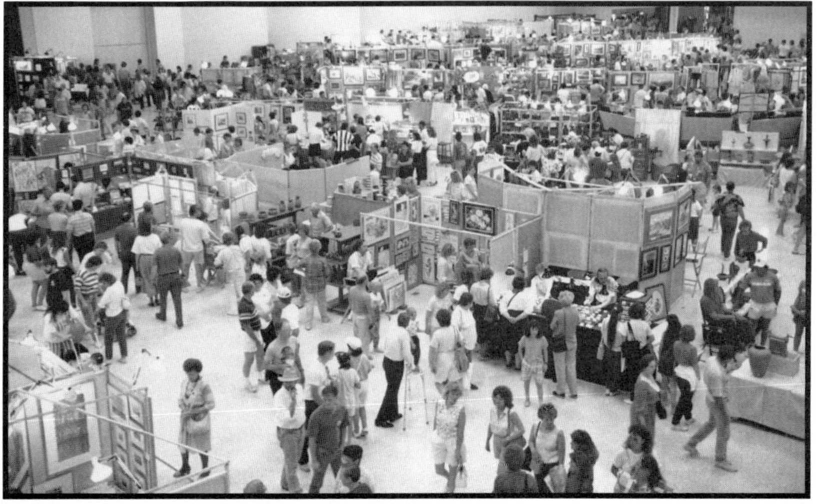

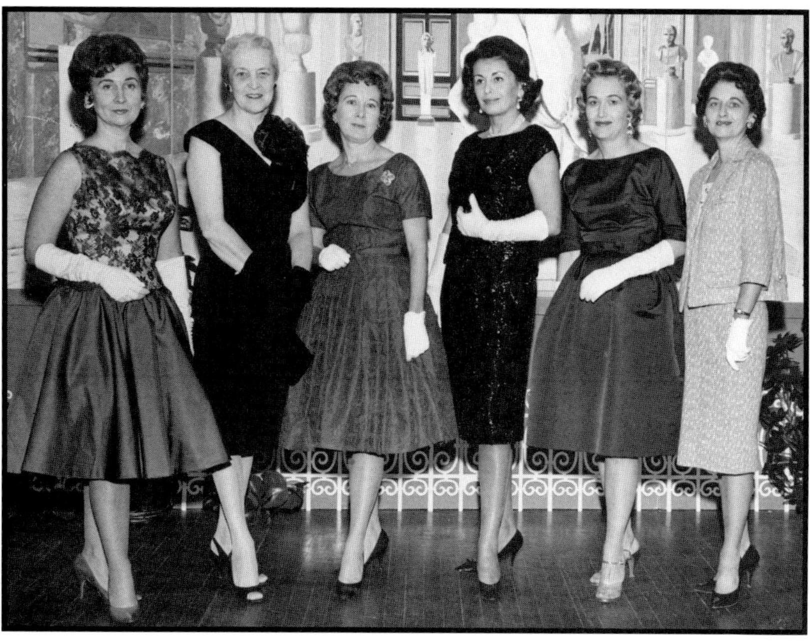

The 1960s brought a series of dances and fashions shows featuring products from other countries to benefit the museum. The events were sponsored by Innes Department Store and the Wichita Art Museum Members. Participants in the 1961 Festival of Italy included, from left to right, Betty Murfin, the first president of WAMM, Jeanne Naugle, Dotti Jeter, Princess Irene Galitzine of Rome, Jean Nelson, and Mrs. A.J. Shirk.

Ginny Malone to announce the goals it proposed: establish membership categories, publish monthly newsletters, institute exhibition previews, sponsor art films, and present a lecture series. In addition, WAMM would sponsor art tours to other museums and provide opportunities for sales or rental of artworks. The featured speaker was Ross Taggart of the Nelson Galleries of Kansas City, Missouri, who described an exhibition of American glass then on loan to the Wichita Art Museum from the Smithsonian Institution.

Director Grove wrote in an April 1961 issue of *Wichita This Week* regarding the Wichita Art Museum Members, Inc.: "I was astounded. . . . They did not sit around discussing Mrs. X's new hat. They went to work. During the first year they accomplished the following:

(1) Presented two series of lectures, an afternoon series on Japanese art and an evening series on American art.
(2) Assembled, installed and paid for an exhibition of Japanese art.
(3) Created a Sales and Rental project for excellent works by Kansas art-

ists or famous artists from galleries in New York. This enterprise is already self-supporting.
(4) Installed a new acoustical ceiling in the Auditorium Gallery. The echo-chamber effect is gone, you can now hear lecturers, film sound tracks . . . .
(5) Sponsored a series of art films which were offered to the public on Sunday afternoon. We could barely squeeze the people in.
(6) Grew to what is now, I believe, the largest such organization in Kansas. They are still adding new members at a fast clip and thinking up extraordinary, interesting new projects for them.

Grove's list of first-year achievements was only the beginning of the support WAMM would provide. The members were innovative and motivated to augment the slim budget allotted the museum by the city. They instituted an annual Book Fair in 1960. It was called the Book and Art Fair the following year and became the Art and Book Fair in the mid-1970s. Its first location was the basement of Mid-Kansas Federal Savings and Loan Association, with Mrs. Howard Menne in charge. Three members, Mrs. Burks Jeter, Mrs. Elbert Naugle, and Mrs. Ralph Drake, had spent two days observing a successful annual book fair benefitting The Nursery Foundation of St. Louis. The early Wichita Book Fairs sold old magazines, sheet music, and records, as well as used books. Works by local artists also were available. But even with the help of the Boy Scouts for transportation and a free location, the first year net was only $400. WAMM persisted, earning $1,000 the second year. In the years to come WAMM would both expand the scope of the fair and further increase its profits.

Another source of funds became available annually from 1961-1966, sponsored by Innes Department Store. Manager Jack Shirk and his successor, Lee Blaser, were committed to improving foreign trade and both endorsed a series of events combining a dinner-dance and fashion show to benefit the Wichita Art Museum. Ticket sales were handled by WAMM and the shows were sellouts. The first was co-sponsored by the Italian Foreign Trade Ministry. Later shows featured export specialties of other areas, including Great Britain, the Mediterranean, France, the Far East, and Scandinavia.

The next endeavor by WAMM was to introduce tours to help visitors appreciate the museum's collections. The new docent program provided trained museum guides, the first of them from the Junior League. As the program expanded, docents came from the community at large. All were trained by the professional staff of the museum. Tours were arranged for both adult groups and public- and parochial-school students under teacher supervision. Docent-led tours continue to be offered.

In 1959 Wichita had no commercial galleries limited solely to paintings. WAMM decided to provide an outlet to display, sell and rent works by local artists, as well as artists of national and international repute. In May 1960 Jayne Milburn chaired the exhibition committee which presented its first sales/rental show with 84 paintings displayed in the museum auditorium. The next two exhibitions were chaired by Virginia Foster and held in the buildings of Mid-Kansas Federal Savings and Loan Association in November 1960, and the Kansas Gas & Electric Company in February 1961. Each show ran for a week. ⁚

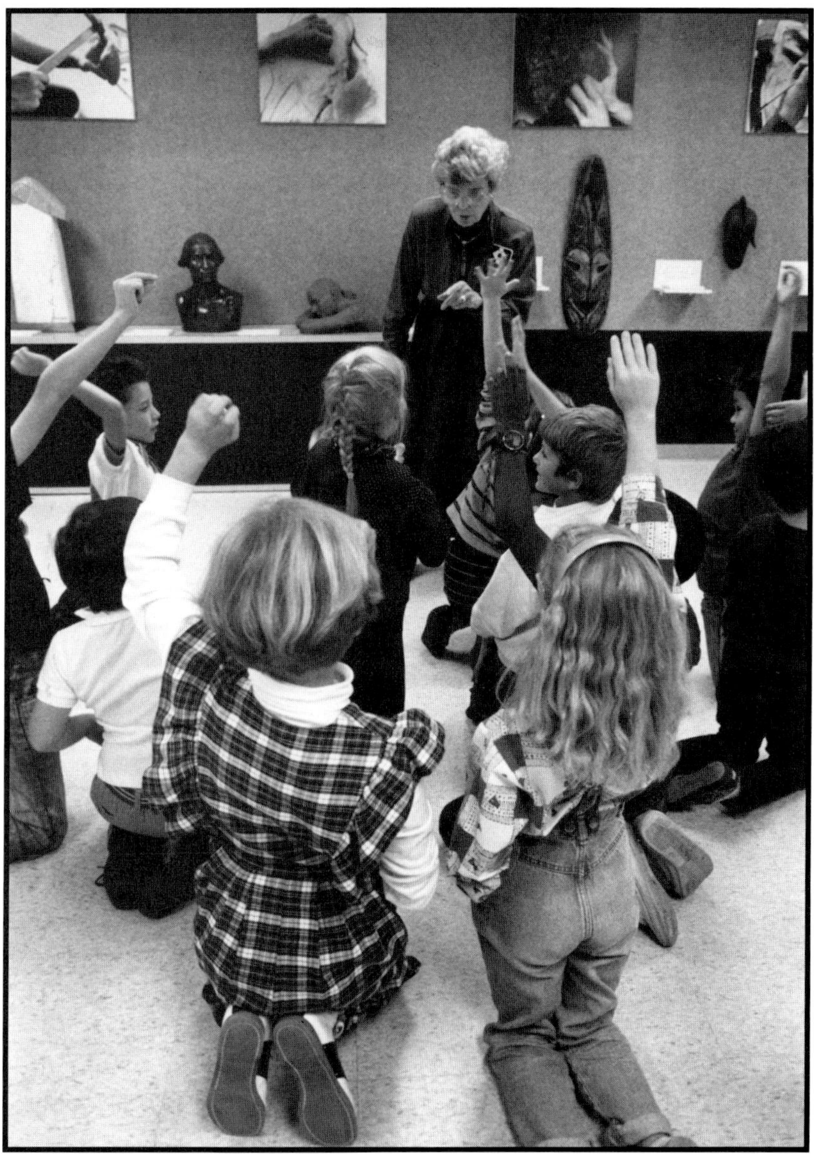

In the early 1960s the Wichita Art Museum Members began a program to train docents who could lead tours of the museum. The program continues today. In this 1989 photograph, docent Ruth Luellen talks with a group of second graders.

Chapter Four
1962-1966

Construction of the Wichita Art Museum's long-needed north and south wings was approved by the City Commission in September 1962. Architect Robert Schaefer's Wichita firm drew the blueprints, which included plans for other improvements. Construction was complete in less than a year and museum activities proceeded without serious disruption. Three collections were assembled

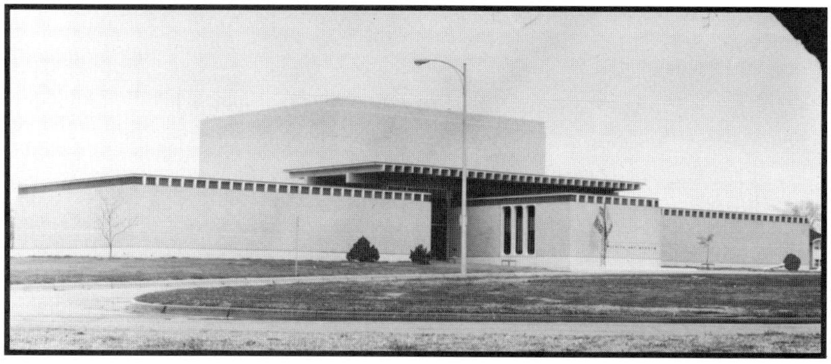

The long-awaited wings of the Wichita Art Museum, completed in 1963, nearly doubled the size of the building.

at the museum and placed there for exhibitions while construction was under way.

The first of these locally-assembled collections was of pre-Columbian art. Attendance at this exhibition in the spring of 1962 was a noteworthy 5,045. Sponsored and assembled by a WAMM committee chaired by Vera Clark and Marjorie Ferguson, the display presented 135 art objects from about 500 B.C. to 1400 A.D. The principal lender to this important exhibition was Haig Kurdian, who provided many pieces from his collection, which later became part of a 468-piece Kurdian gift to the Wichita Art Museum.

The second of these three exhibitions, *Indian Art of the Southwest*, was designed to give an idea of the range and depth of Southwestern Indian art. An advisory group of collectors, artists, and scholars helped bring together examples of superb quality in basketry, jewelry, weaving, embroidery, pottery, carving, and sand painting. Margaret Bradley, a collector of Indian artworks, chaired the museum's

sponsoring committee and wrote the exhibition catalogue. A series of lectures on Indian art was given between November 1962 and February 1963 before the opening of the exhibition on February 26.

Rounding out the exhibition schedule, *The A B C's of Art* was designed for first-through 12th-grade students. The Junior League and museum members pooled talents for the project, which opened in March 1963 and continued through May. Materials were donated by local businesses and a special gift came from artist Barbara Mallonee, chairman of the exhibition. She designed and illustrated a booklet for distribution to all local elementary schools. Called *The A B C's of Art, the FUNdamentals*, it depicted the basic elements of art and explained to young people how to find these elements in their surroundings and how to use them when drawing or painting.

Renovation work began in early 1963. Opening ceremonies were conducted at noon on October 6, 1963, by Mayor Gerald S. Byrd, accompanied by Schuyler Crawford, president of the Park Board. Others on hand included Jayne Milburn, chairman of the Wichita Art Museum board; Jo Kitch, president of the Wichita Art Museum Members; Richard Grove, museum director; and Mildred Armstrong, president of the Junior League, Inc., of Wichita. The league underwrote an exhibition to celebrate the occasion. Circulated by the American Federation of Arts, the exhibition was titled *The Road to Impressionism*. The ribbon-cutting ceremonies and an official museum tour were given television coverage courtesy of the University of Wichita's Educational Television Department.

A proud moment followed when the doors to the museum's new entrance were flung open. The building's improvements were evident at once in the spacious foyer and wide openings to the north and south wings. Here at last was a museum that looked like one. Visitors found notably increased gallery space within the 10,000 square feet added in the expansion. They found a small library that could double as a board room, its appointments furnished by the Junior League. There were new administrative offices and a small office for WAMM and its first salaried secretary, Evelyn Melby.

In the meantime, a 1962 decision by the Kansas Supreme Court ended a two-year dispute between the Murdock trustees and Sedgwick County regarding the tax status of the Caldwell-Murdock Building, the source of the Murdock Trust's income. The court returned the building to the property-tax rolls. It had been off the rolls since 1938, when the Sedgwick County District Court decreed an exemption because income from the building was used for civic purposes, according to newspaper accounts. The Sedgwick County assessor argued that the building should be returned to the tax rolls because it was being operated for profit and in competition with other office buildings.

The Supreme Court ruling came as an unexpected blow to the museum, for it effectively stopped growth of the Murdock Collection. Murdock trustee Garner Shriver explained during the dispute that it would take virtually all the trust's income to pay the annual tax bill.

The unwelcome court decree of 1962 was a signal to Wichita civic leaders that their art museum needed help beyond that which the loyal WAMM could supply. In the same year, 14 men chaired by Philip Kassebaum offered their services as a council of advisers to the museum director. In 1964 another subsidiary board was named. It was called the Wichita Art Museum Members Foundation and absorbed the older WAMM. When requested to combine names and hand over its articles of incorporation, WAMM regretted its loss of identity but complied. In 1965 the unincorporated council of advisers also moved under the corporate umbrella of the new Wichita Art Museum Members Foundation, Inc.

Richard Grove resigned in January 1964 to join the Cultural Affairs Branch of the United States Office of Education in Washington, D.C. His departure moved assistant Sebastian Adler to the post of acting director and then, in November, to the director's office. Adler had come in 1963 from Sioux Falls, Minnesota, where he founded and directed the Civic Arts Center. A graduate of Minnesota's state college at Winona, Mr. Adler had taught

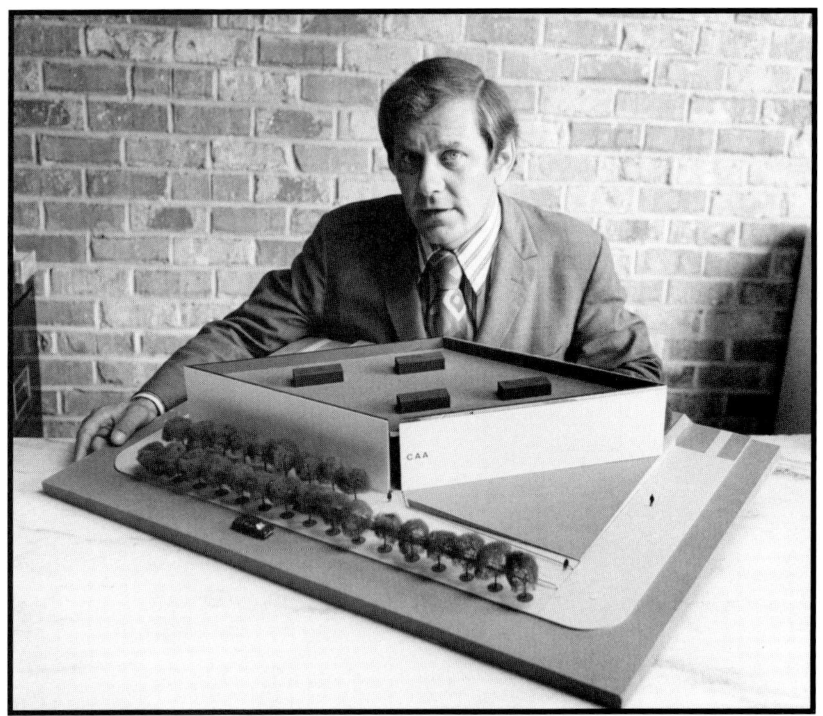

art for three years at Worthington and founded the Nobels County Art Center there.

The first exhibition under Adler's direction came in the spring of 1965. *The American Home of the Colonial and Federal Periods* was a display of furniture and furnishings borrowed from local households. Although not a large show, it was popular because of the quality and variety of long-cherished heirlooms. Ross E.

Sebastian Adler, who became director of the museum in 1964, was fired by the museum board and promptly rehired by the City Commission as 'Protector of Art.'

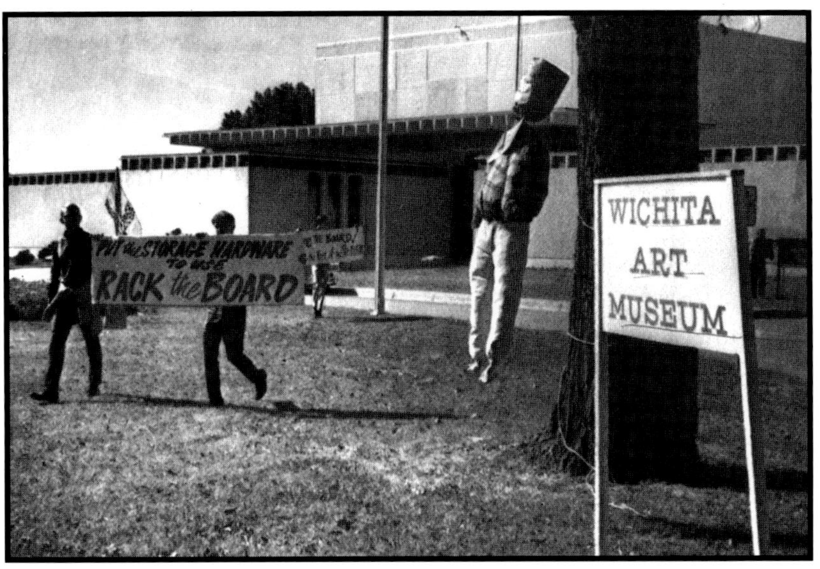

Demonstrators marched in front of the museum in October 1965 to protest the firing of museum director Sebastian Adler. Wichita Eagle photo

Taggart from the Nelson Gallery in Kansas City served as consultant to the Wichita Art Museum's Exhibition Committee, co-chaired by Mary Ellen Barrier and Jeane Yankey. Assisted by Wichita Art Museum Curator Jon Nelson, the committee assembled, selected, and arranged the pieces in 12 bays constructed to partially encircle the main gallery.

Everything appeared to be proceeding smoothly until dissatisfactions regarding certain of Adler's exhibition plans and actions were voiced within the museum board. Little of this reached beyond the board room, so it came as a shock when the board broke the silence with notices of emergency actions to take place on the evening of October 21, 1965. A closed meeting of the board was called for 7 p.m. in the museum library. Adler was summoned to appear there at 7:15 and the boards of both the old WAMM and the new Wichita Art Museum Members Foundation were requested to join for another meeting in the auditorium at 7:30. Attendance was overwhelming. Tension was so high, speculation so unrestrained, that one member recalled having been advised by her husband to find a seat next to a reliable friend who could help "keep her in it."

Patience had worn thin by the time museum board Chairman Vera Clark came from the closed library to tell the restless waiting audience that Director Sebastian Adler had just been fired. The meager explanation that he had exceeded his authority left many questions, and when the meeting broke up members were in turmoil. Mr. Adler was quoted in the next morning's *Wichita Eagle* as having told a reporter, "They didn't give me any reason, just that I was discharged – I didn't know what their reason is."

In the days immediately following, opinion polarized. Students from the art departments of Wichita State and Friends universities picketed the art museum on Tuesday, October 26. The City Commission's regularly scheduled 9 a.m. meeting took place before a packed chamber that morning. That evening's *Wichita Beacon* reported that the City Commission had appointed Sebastian Adler to serve the museum under contract in a newly created interim position as "Protector of Art." *The Beacon* also described "an early breakfast meeting called by Mayor William Tarrant" on the 26th before the regular public meeting at which "the five City Commissioners repeatedly asked Museum Board members for specific reasons why Adler was fired. They got only general answers contained in a prepared statement. . . . among other things it said that he had made erroneous representations to the Board."

While naming Adler "Protector of Art," the commission accepted the resignations of five members of the museum board that had fired him. The commission named these replacements: Chairman Paul Woods, Mary Ellen Barrier, Dr. George Mastio, Austin Rising, and Martin Umansky. Richard Harris and Walter Merrill were retained. Six months later Mr. Woods reminded his board, "We have never technically rehired Mr. Adler. As chairman I have found him very cooperative and move that the board rehire Mr.

Adler as museum director and that the board reassume responsibility for the position." The board unanimously approved the motion. Adler remained until June 1966, when he resigned to become director of the Houston (Texas) Museum of Contemporary Arts.

A new endeavor began in 1966, sponsored by the Wichita Art Museum Members' Foundation and Unified School District No. 354 in Medicine Lodge, Kansas. It was a traveling art display for schools in rural areas. Kansas Gas and Electric Company of Wichita donated a truck and trailer that were remodeled into a mobile gallery called the Artmobile, which could show 17 to 20 items at each stop. Two displays per year were sent to public and parochial schools in nine southcentral Kansas counties. Operating expenses were paid through a Title III federal grant and a Sears Roebuck Foundation grant. Local artist Blackbear Bosin designed and donated a colorful logo for the van.

Guidebooks were written and sent to teachers in advance of the Artmobile's arrival. These books included details on the available teaching materials, including slides and film strips. Marcia Schoenberg served in a curatorial capacity on the museum staff. Marian Beren, project chairman for WAMM and vice president of the Foundation, and the young mobile gallery curators made important contributions to the long-term success of the program.

After a brief dedication ceremony on the morning of November 16, 1966, the van was opened for public viewing for a few days. Then Richard Miller, the Artmobile's first curator, took it on the road and reported good response from students, teachers, and parents.

A larger van would be put on the road in 1968, the program would be expanded, and the geographical reach extended to other parts of the state. In 1969 the federal funding would end and would be replaced by the Kansas Arts Commission, with a fee required from the schools served. By September 1980 the program would be reorganized and renamed the "Traveling Visual Arts Program" (TVAP), developed by the Wichita Art Museum under a grant from the Kansas Arts Commission. The visual arts program of the 1980s would involve statewide circulation of a series of fine art exhibitions. Its goal would be to offer Kansas communities an opportunity to display a wide variety of educational and aesthetically pleasing exhibitions to audiences of all ages at a modest cost. &

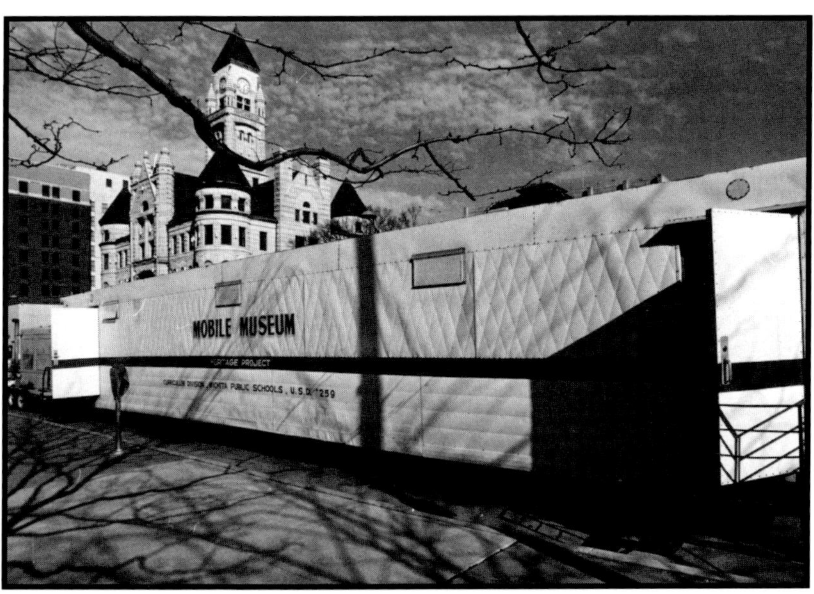

The museum's Artmobile began taking displays on the road to rural schools in 1966. The 1977 version of the traveling museum is shown here. Wichita Eagle photo

CHAPTER FIVE

1967-1971

Director Sebastian Adler's departure in 1966 brought his curator John Petty to the acting directorship of the museum. Within the next year and a half, Petty arranged for two well-received exhibitions. The first, *Wyeth's World*, a gift funded by the Junior League, Inc., of Wichita, brought a collection of 52 Andrew Wyeth paintings to the museum during September 1967. This was an especially popular show that set attendance records. The second exhibition, *Masterpieces of Religious Art*, included 55 works of European art

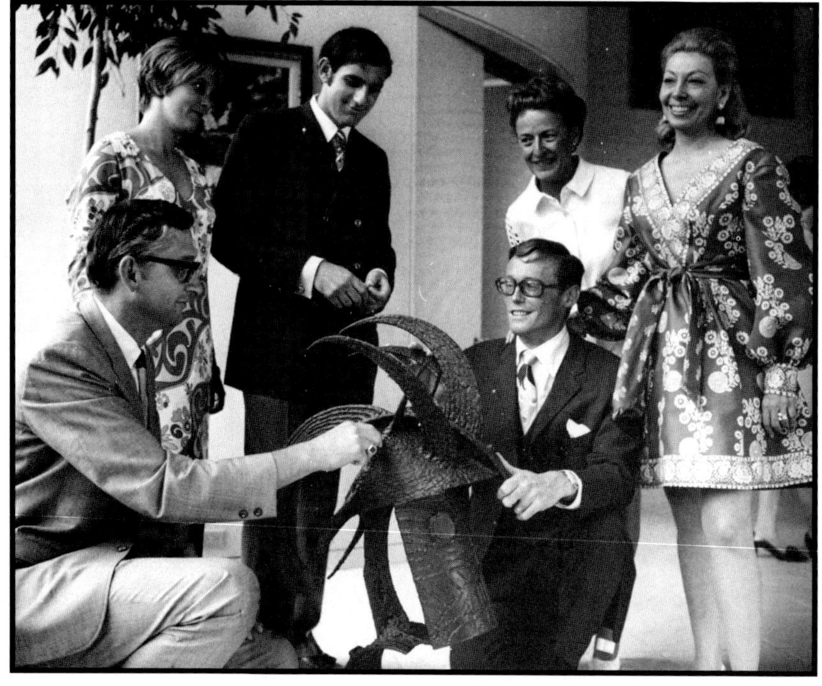

Richard Teitz, who became director of the museum in 1967, was succeeded by Jan von Adlmann in 1969. Shown here at a reception are, left to right, Paul Hampel, Mrs. Teitz, Mr. Teitz, Mr. von Adlmann, Ginny Malone, and Marian Chuzy.

dating from the mid-15th to the mid-18th century. The loans came from 27 sources. Mr. Petty missed the opportunity to preside at the opening in December 1967 by accepting the directorship of the Washington County Museum in Hagerstown, Maryland. He moved there in September, the same month that Richard Teitz arrived in Wichita to assume his appointment as museum director.

Mr. Teitz, a native of Newport, Rhode Island, received his bachelor of arts degree from Yale and a master's degree from Harvard. He had been on the staff of the

Fogg Art Museum and had held teaching positions at the Boston Architectural Center and at Clark University in Worcester, Massachusetts. He remained in Wichita for two years before returning to Massachusetts to become assistant director of the Worcester Art Museum.

The second of the Wichita Art Museum's exhibitions of *The American Home* series, *Art of the Victorian Era*, was presented in May and June 1968. Like the first, this exhibition displayed items on loan from local sources. Director Teitz paid tribute in the preface of the exhibition catalogue to the work of the Members Committee's chairmen, Nancy Kassebaum (now a U.S. senator) and Jeanne Yankey "who diligently and knowledgeably selected the exhibition and compiled the catalogue."

Wichita Collects, a 1969 exhibition assembled in Wichita to mark the celebration of the city's 100th anniversary, demonstrated both the scope and quality of works of art owned in the community. It was planned under the direction of Richard Teitz with the assistance of three friends of the museum, Pamela Kingsbury, assistant curator; George Vollmer, a collector; and Ginny Malone, WAMM president. These three Wichita natives knew where to find the city's fine paintings and how to obtain their temporary loan.

The June 25, 1969, *Wichita Eagle* noted that "The Wichita Art Museum has gained and lost. Its gain in the form of 14 [recent] acquisitions . . . . Its loss is the resignation of Richard Teitz, the 24-year-old museum director and the man most responsible for the acquisitions." He would be remembered as an early advocate for putting a new Wichita Art Museum on the planning agenda of the City Commission.

Teitz was succeeded by Jan von Adlmann. Mr. von Adlmann's bachelor's degree from the University of Maine had brought with it a Phi Beta Kappa key. His master's from New York University's Institute of Fine Arts had brought fellowships to the University of Vienna and the University of West Berlin. On September 1, 1969, he came to the Wichita Art Museum from his position as director of the Tampa Bay (Florida) Art Center. Because the timing of his arrival coincided closely with the arrival of a Ford Foundation grant, work already begun on a Murdock Collection catalogue by Richard Teitz was completed by von Adlmann.

Von Adlmann's own *tour de force* was the museum's exhibition of junk trivia in the fall of 1970. Titled *Kitsch, the Grotesque Around Us*, it was a jolting surprise planned to demonstrate the lamentable abundance of poor design, faulty execution, and bad taste in commercial production. With its examples of "visual pollution," the exhibition drew attention well beyond its original setting. The Phoenix Art Museum, the Delgado in New Orleans, and the Colorado Springs Art Center sent inquiries about rental arrangements. *Time* magazine and national art publications took note, and five cities presented the exhibition.

With the 1970s came the exciting prospect of a new museum building. Enthusiasm was renewed. The Wichita Art Museum Members Foundation, with its creative resources committee chaired by Mrs. William (Mary Jo) Malone, turned out the town for a grand fund-raising, fun-making extravaganza on March 18, 1970, dubbed *Farewell to the Miller*. The departing "Miller," an aging Wichita theater, was awaiting the wrecker's ball, and the "Farewell" was a nostalgic review of the theater's early days. Anecdotes from its latter-day, one-night revival are told by Ginny Malone:

Our purpose was to raise money to purchase paintings for the museum.

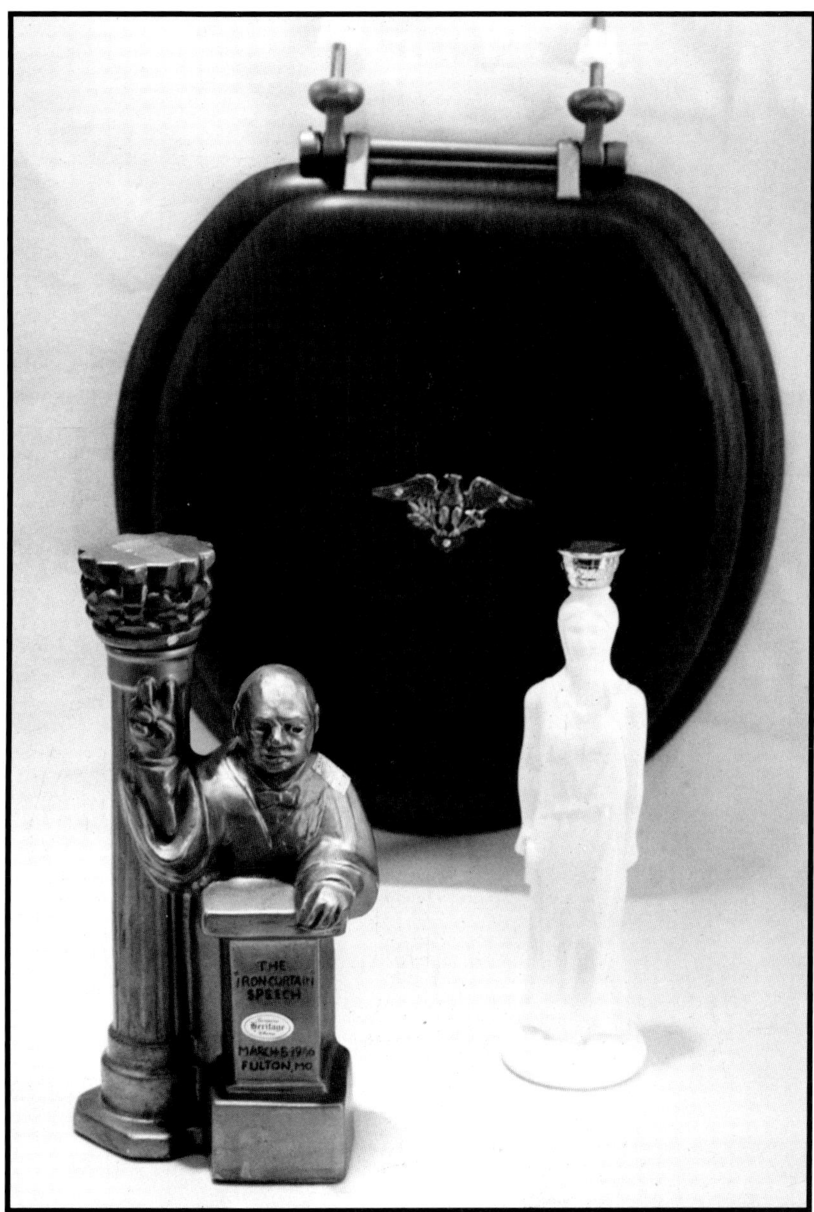

Involved in this successful project was almost every member of the museum and its staff, non-members, past employees of the Miller Theater, and local dignitaries. Indeed, thinking back, I'm surprised there were enough participants in the Wichita area to fill every seat in the largest theater west of the Missouri and to give us a handsome profit.

The third and final presentation of the

Director Jan von Adlmann is best remembered for putting together Kitsch, the Grotesque Around Us, *a 1970 exhibition that traveled to five cities.*

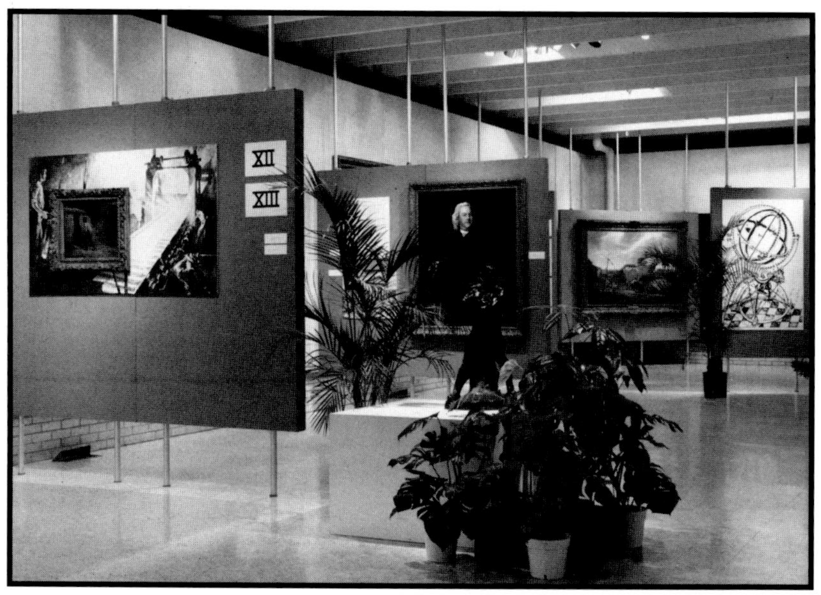

Civilisation Re-Visited: An Homage to Sir Kenneth Clark, *an exhibition in 1971, included such works as Rembrandt's* Head of Christ *and Rodin's* Honore de Balzac.

of Interior Design. The exhibition centered upon a wheel 48 feet in diameter as a basic classic design, and used a circle-with-spokes floor plan to demarcate eight displays.

The widely-acclaimed film series "Civilisation," based on Sir Kenneth Clark's opus and presented by public television in 1971, became the touchstone for a collection of more than 55 paintings, drawings, and sculptures. This collection engaged the support of the Wichita Art Museum, the Board of Education, four local foundations, four corporations, a trust fund and several private citizens in an effort called *Civilisation Re-Visited: An Homage to Sir Kenneth Clark.* The artworks came on loan from 29 art institutions and several private collections, and included Rembrandt's *Head of Christ,* Rodin's *Honore de Balzac,* Durer's *Melancholia* and Monet's *House of Parliament, London.* The exhibition in December 1971 was described by von Adlmann as "one of the most important programs the Art Museum has ever undertaken." The museum rented a double-deck bus for free transportation of students to and from the museum. ❧

Museum's *American Home* series, *Classic Designs for Living,* was exhibited in September 1971. Using the term "classic" in the broadest sense, this exhibit focused on both antique and modern examples which embodied Greek and Roman designs. As in the earlier exhibits, all items were on loan from Wichita homes. Barbara Mallonee chaired this WAMM undertaking with the assistance of a number of local members of the American Institute

In 1971 about 100 young people who shared an interest in the Wichita Art Museum came together in a group called "The Young at 'Art." Their focus was on good fellowship and learning in the pleasant ambience of the museum. Their evening meetings began in January 1972 with Max Schaible as president. One of these featured a lecture by Jim Avant of Wichita State University's art department on collages as an art form. In March the group prepared and hosted a reception for the museum's opening of a Sears-sponsored exhibition of antique toys. Attendance at the museum's Sunday afternoon foreign films was swelled by "The Young at 'Art." They also contributed to the Art and Book Fairs of 1972 and 1973 by offering a supervised children's activity center. Unfortunately, in 1973 when all program scheduling faced curtailments because of the museum's upcoming reconstruction, "The Young at 'Art" quietly faded from the changing scene at the museum.

An important addition to the museum's collections came as a gift from the Naftzger family in 1973. The 18 works by Charles M. Russell, chronicler of the Old West, include paintings, sculptures, and illustrations.

Assurance of a new museum building came in 1973 when the Wichita City Commission allocated $3.5 million from Community Development Act funding. Attention turned to the location. Should it be built on the original site or on one of five others thought worthy of consideration? It soon became evident that this matter would not be readily or easily settled. The controversy used up a great deal of time, newsprint, and patience. Commissioner John Stevens clung doggedly to his first and only choice, the original museum location, and he threatened to call a referendum whenever that choice was challenged. Others pointed to the risk of losing the new building altogether if delays over the location continued. The commission finally hired an outside consultant, the Washington, D.C., firm of Gutheim, Seligman and Erickson, which sent Frederick Gutheim to Wichita. His first choice was a downtown site near Century II. Most of the commissioners had earlier agreed to propose the site as a trial balloon. The proposal was sent to the newspapers, only to arouse a storm of public protest over predicted parking problems.

During the same period the museum

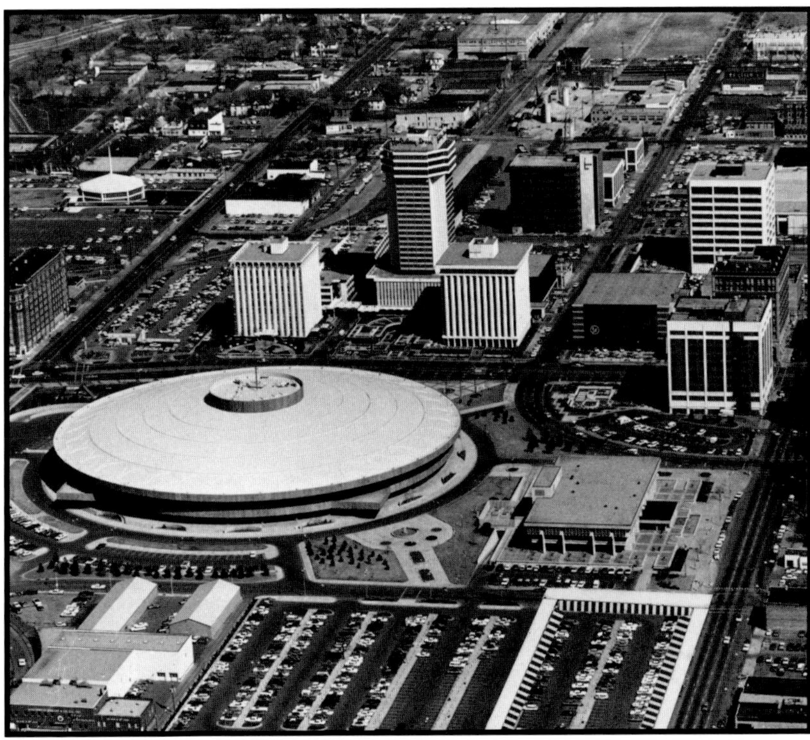

board also faced finding a new director to replace Jan von Adlmann, who had resigned on December 1, 1972, to become director of the Long Beach (California) Museum of Art. It appeared that a director had been found when Sue McWhirter Thurman agreed to come to Wichita from her position as chairman of Rutgers University's Douglas College Department of Art in New Jersey. However, before Mrs. Thurman had time to settle into her new job she was beset by a serious health problem that required her to resign. On April 15, 1973, George Vollmer, a strong museum

Among the sites considered for a new museum in 1973 was one near Century II, shown in the lower right corner of this photograph. Other sites were eventually rejected in favor of the existing location on Stackman Drive. Wichita Eagle photo

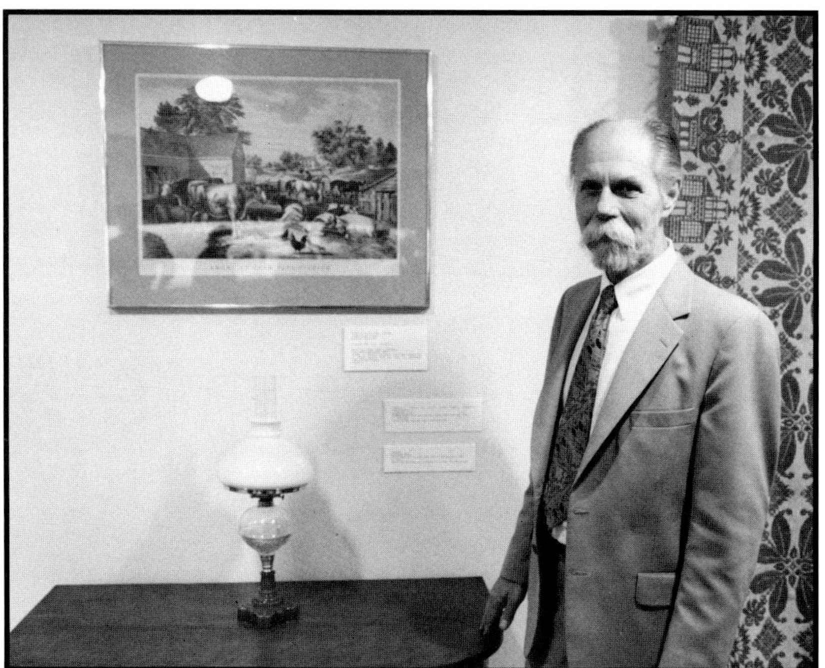

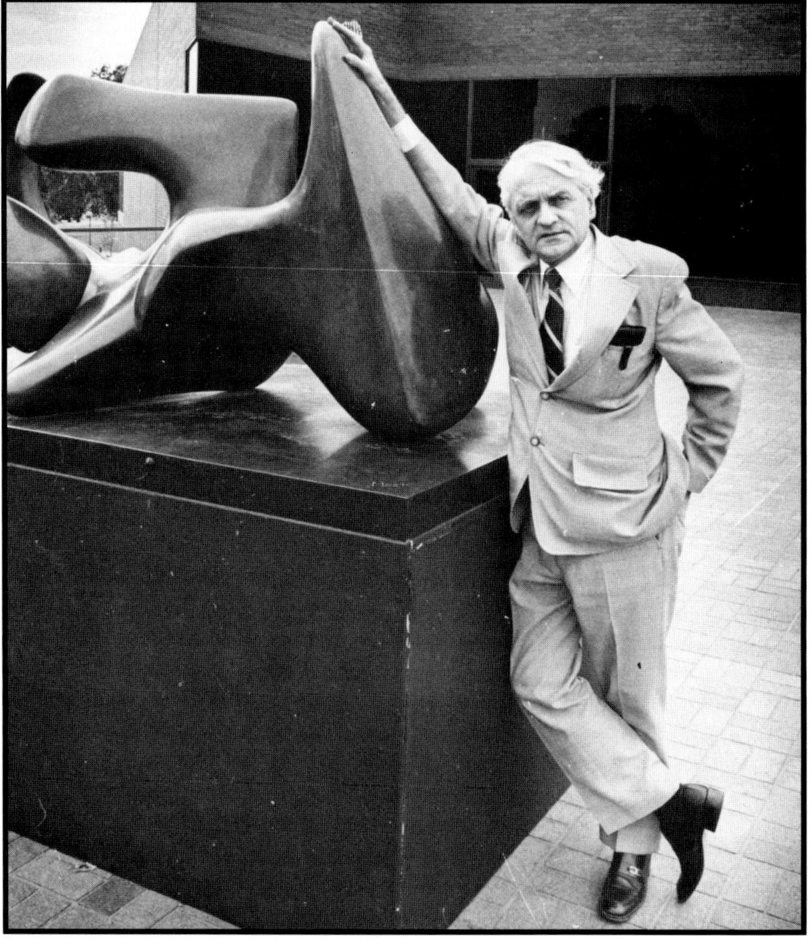

supporter with serious art interests, had been persuaded to fill in as acting director for the interval prior to Mrs. Thurman's arrival in August, and he stepped in again after her departure in October.

As a condition of accepting the position, Mr. Vollmer insisted that the board hire consultants to discuss two issues: the new site for the museum and the board's role in the functioning of the museum. Three consultants were invited to meet with the museum board on successive weekends in March 1974: Richard McClanathan, a noted art museum consultant recognized for architectural expertise; George Seybold, president-emeritus of the Boston Fine Arts Museum; and Kyran McGrath, executive director of the American Association of Museums.

Downtown parking problems and land costs forced reconsideration of the Century II site. Another serious look was taken at the existing Stackman Drive site. The second group of consultants had already determined that museum members in general preferred this location and were not opposed to a large-scale reconstruction of the old building to hold down costs. However, this arrangement would not comply with an Urban Renewal requirement that funding be applied only to "new" buildings.

Don Anderson, city director of administration, proposed a compromise. Believing that the museum would be entitled to use city funds if the building were "reconstructed" or "remodeled," Anderson requested a legal opinion. With the confirmation of Anderson's judgment, the commissioners were finally able to act.

"At last a decision has been reached (by the City Commission) on the new Art Museum," said *The Wichita Eagle-Beacon's* lead editorial on August 28, 1974. "It will be built at the present location on Stackman Drive." Wichita enjoyed a sigh of relief. Meanwhile, the museum's board braced for further decisions of its own: finding a new administrator for a museum whose building would soon be in large part demolished; searching for interim headquarters for the two-year reconstruction period; and selecting architectural and construction firms.

By December 1974, three prominent New York-based architects experienced in art museum design were recognized as the leading candidates: Phillip Johnson, Edward Larrabee Barnes, and I.M. Pei. After careful deliberation, the museum board appointed Mr. Barnes designer and chose the Wichita architectural firm of Platt, Adams and Braht to execute and manage the project. The Law Company of Wichita was later awarded the construction contract.

In the spring of 1975, Howard Wooden resigned as director of the Sheldon Swope Art Gallery in Terre Haute, Indiana, to become director of the Wichita Art Museum. A native of Baltimore, Maryland, he had earned his bachelor's and master's degrees with arts and archaeology majors at Johns Hopkins University. Before assuming his post at Terre Haute, Mr. Wooden had been a Fulbright instructor in Greece, and thereafter an associate professor in the art departments at the University of Florida and Indiana State University.

The new director's abilities as an art historian and lecturer became evident within weeks of his arrival in August 1975. Almost immediately he offered a fall monthly lecture series, followed by a series of art appreciation tours on Sunday afternoons.

At the time of Wooden's arrival, four urgent administrative issues faced the museum. The first involved the completion of architectural plans and specifications for the new museum building. The second concerned the need to establish an exhibition program for the five months or so prior to the beginning of construction. The third was the selection of temporary quarters for the two-year construction period. The main objectives were to have adequate and secure space for work, storage and exhibitions. These features were readily found when, with the cooperation of one of the museum's long-time friends, Harry Litwin, the trust department of the vacated Fourth National Bank building at Douglas and Market streets

was made available. The spacious storage vaults of the former bank offered security comparable to that of any modern museum. Moreover, temperature and humidity met requirements for the protection of art objects.

The fourth problem, which dominated the fall of 1975 and early winter of 1976, concerned the move to the temporary quarters, several miles away in the center of town. The plans involved detailed arrangements for the transfer of all equipment, office supplies, furniture, files, text books, and journals. All works of art had to be securely crated for transport and indexed for long-term storage and easy retrieval for exhibitions. Staff members spent five months planning this phase. In six days, January 5 through January 10, 1976, what came to be known as "Operation Museum Move" was undertaken in closed vans under armed guard and without incident. Two weeks later, the temporary museum opened to the public. A few days later, on January 27, ground-breaking ceremonies for the new museum were held. Much of the old building was quickly demolished; the new would be completed two years later. &

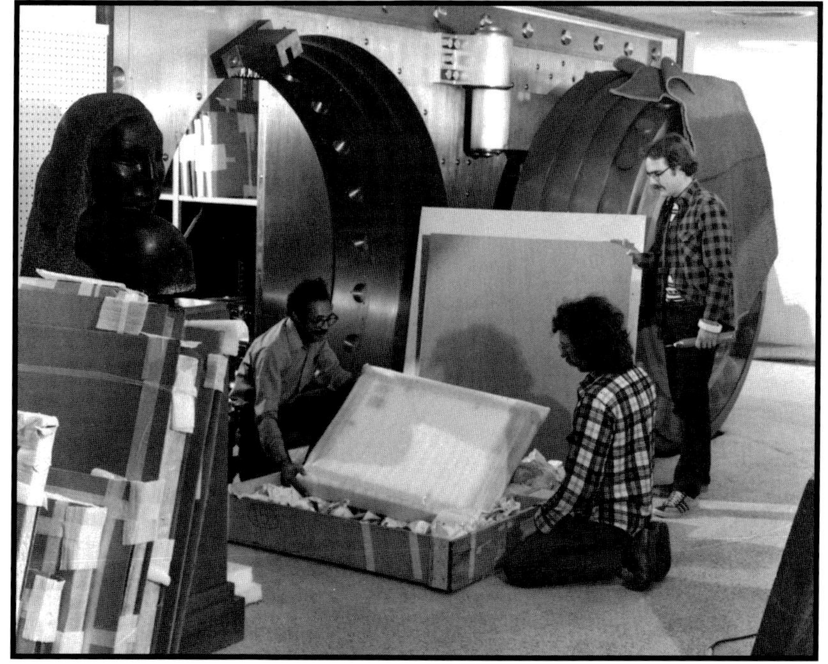

Below: When reconstruction of the museum on Stackman Drive began in 1976, the museum's collections moved to a former bank building downtown. The vault was used for storage and the rooms and hallways for galleries.

CHAPTER SEVEN
1976-1979

Just before the old building at 619 Stackman Drive was abandoned to the demolition and construction crews, "last rites" arranged by Ginny Malone were administered on the evening of January 10, 1976. About 250 people attended. Special features included a "paint-in" resulting in 40 Hasty Masterpieces; a One-Man Show of Edible Art for Purchase, Not for Rent; a Brick Boutique, selling souvenir bricks for $1 and lucky bricks containing gifts for $5; and a Valuable Art Auction to augment funds for the purchase of a nude by Philip Pearlstein. On hand was an enlarged copy of the Pearlstein painting from which various parts were individually offered for sale. Dr. Charles Rombold, who had proposed the idea, stood by in a surgeon's gown and accomplished the sectioning. Bidding was lively and so were auctioneer Max Schaible's running comments.

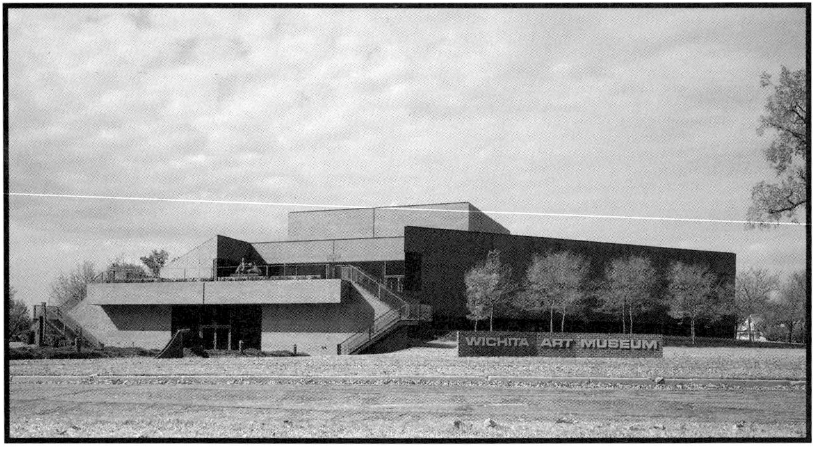

The new museum, designed by Edward Larrabee Barnes, opened in 1977. It incorporates portions of the original building.

Soon afterward the museum was open to the public at its temporary downtown location in the Litwin Building. Because of the low ceilings, the exhibitions were restricted to relatively small-scale paintings and prints, yet programming was extensive. Many of the exhibitions were planned with an educational focus for student audiences. The downtown location was well received and regularly visited.

During the entire two years, a high level of enthusiasm prevailed among board members and the staff. The director's Friday morning staff meetings included progress reports with slide illustrations of the changes taking place at the building site. Later there were staff tours of the growing building.

"THE WICHITA ART MUSEUM RE-OPENS" was the heading of the museum's October 1977 *Newsletter.* Forty-two years had passed since the city's original art museum building had been dedicated. Even now in the building's third and latest architectural phase, two areas of the first could be easily identified in the handsome rotunda[5] and the auditorium. These areas were skillfully blended into the new structure, which spoke eloquently for the architect Edward Larrabee Barnes, for the local architects who supported him, and for the members of the museum board of 1974-1975 who appointed him.

The inaugural exhibition, titled *Five Thousand Years of Art from the Metropolitan Museum of Art,* comprised 78 art objects. All the works were selected by Howard Wooden with the cooperation and assistance of the Metropolitan's director and curatorial staff. In his introduction to the exhibition's catalogue, Mr. Wooden wrote: "The exhibition itself tells a dramatically impressive story of human achievement over a period of more than 5,000 years."

The formal public reopening ceremony came on Sunday, October 23, with an afternoon ribbon-cutting shared by Mayor A.F. "Tony" Casado and Museum Board President Lulu Brasted, and a dedication speech by the director. Dora Timmerman was in charge of preparations for guided tours of the building. Elizabeth Navas, who had selected much of the museum's permanent collection as trustee of the Murdock estate, was among those attending.

The expanded museum included new galleries on the first, second, and lower levels; a board room named in honor of Lulu Brasted, president of the board of directors during the planning and construction; the Gwendolyn Houston Naftzger Lounge, where the Naftzger gift of Boehm and Doughty birds is a permanent display; the Kurdian Gallery named in honor of the family whose gifts of pre-Columbian artifacts and Syrian glass are often displayed there; the M.C. Naftzger Gallery, which presents the Naftzger Collection of Charles M. Russell paintings, drawings and small bronzes.

In contrast with the tiny, crowded library in the original museum and the inviting reading room of the second, the library of the new building was designed to accommodate private study carrels to allow staff or docents to engage in research. The library is not open to the public, but is available to students, teachers, and qualified visitors who apply at the museum's Office of Education.

The outdoor sculpture deck, visible through the building from its main entrance on the second level, was named for Dan and Frank Carney, the Wichita founders of the internationally-known Pizza Hut restaurant chain. In their honor the heroically-proportioned Henry Moore bronze, *Vertebrae No. III*, was installed on the sculpture deck as a gift to the museum from "Friends and Franchisees of Pizza Hut." Additional sculptures on the deck include Richard Hunt's *Extended Land Form*, a combined gift from the Fourth National Bank Foundation, Mr. and Mrs. Kenneth P. Brasted, Sr., Mr. Harry Litwin and an anonymous donor, and John Silk Deckard's *Knife Man*, an eight-foot cast bronze, donated in 1977 from the Wichita Art Museum Members Purchase Fund.

Another welcomed addition to the museum was the River Room, a spacious multi-purpose area named for its fine view of a bend in the Little Arkansas River. The

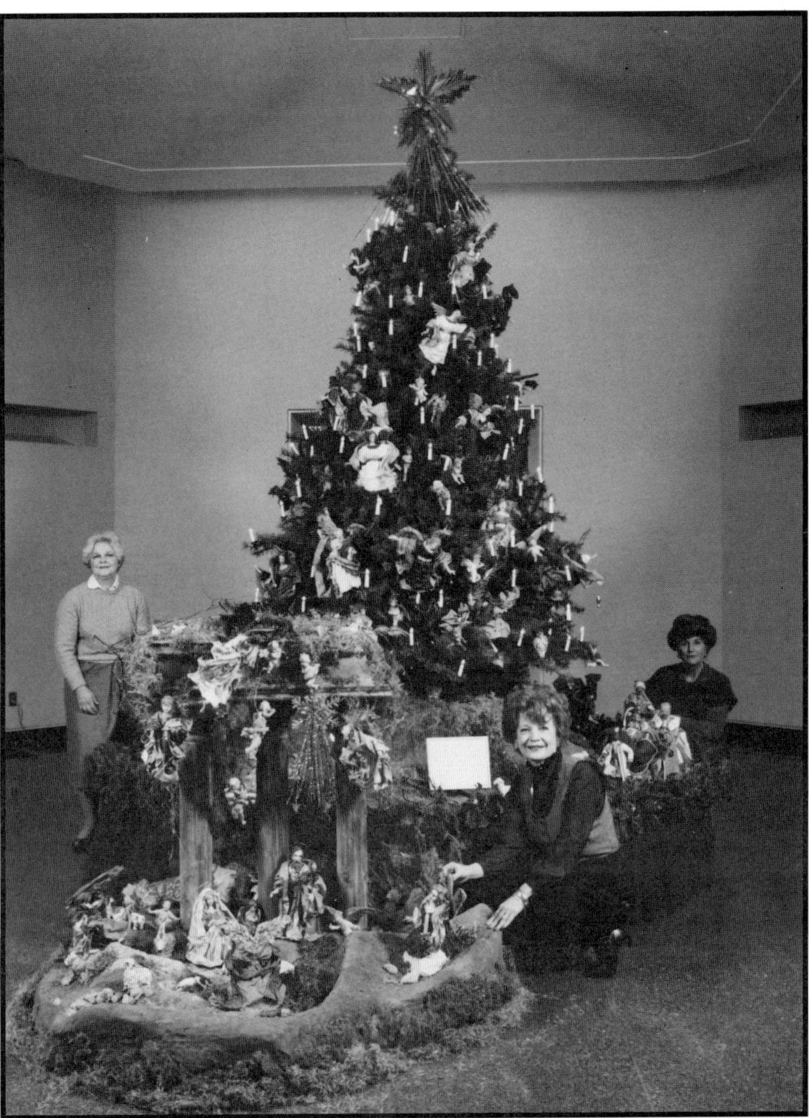

room accommodates a range of museum functions and, for a short time in early December each year, it becomes fragrantly forested with Christmas greens for an event known as *Holidays at the Art Museum.*

The year 1979 brought a unique contribution to the annual holiday display, a large Christmas tree decorated in the manner of the still larger tree exhibited each year at the Metropolitan Museum. Barbara Rensner persuaded sculptors Babs Mellor, Carlene Banks, and Marge Rine that they could achieve a similar effect on a smaller scale. The three volunteers worked for a year to prepare angel figures which, like the 17th and 18th century Neapolitan originals in New York, are beautifully made and richly robed. Since its first appearance, "The Tree of Joy" was returned annually to the museum rotunda through

The 'Tree of Joy' was added to the museum's annual holiday celebration in 1979. Sculptors Carlene Banks, left, Babs Mellor, and Marge Rine made the angels for the tree and the nativity figures at the base.

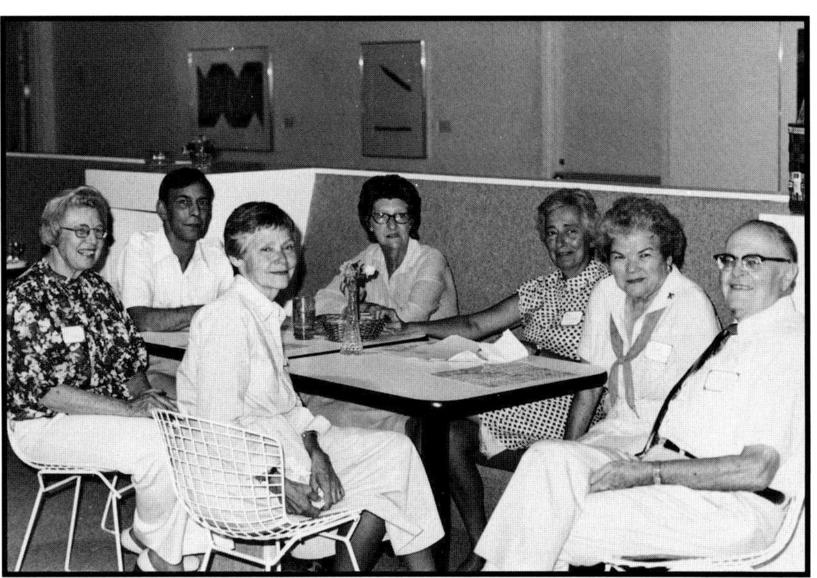

The museum restaurant began as an all-volunteer effort, led by the first co-chairmen, Ruth Coultis and Jean Heckelman. Among the hundreds of volunteers who have helped are, left to right, Bertha Milbank, Bobby Brown, Jo Weaver, Virginia Wooden, Fran Aitchison, Marie Findlay, and Ralph Stewart.

1989, enhanced by newer angels and nativity figures at its base.

From the earliest planning, a restaurant, a gift shop, and a place for the successful sales/rental gallery had been envisioned for the new building. Each began operating soon after the museum's October opening and all three are have become valuable assets to the museum.

The restaurant's first co-chairmen were Ruth Coultis and Jean Heckelman, who made the restaurant available as a coffee shop during museum hours. Varying schedules were tried as the volunteer crews were organized to serve lunch five days a week. Credit goes to hundreds of women and men who sustained this service.

As part of Wichita's sister-city relationship with Orleans, France, an exhibition on loan from Orleans opened May 14, 1978, at the Wichita Art Museum. It included 88 French artists' paintings, prints, drawings, and sculptures. Along with the art, the French had shipped 15 cases of wine to be served at a party celebrating the opening of the exhibition. Unfortunately, the wine was impounded by the United States Customs Service pending clearance from the Kansas Alcoholic Beverage Control Division in Topeka because there was no provision in Kansas law for the city to pay either the federal or state taxes.

While Wichita dealt with this protocol puzzle, the wine was warming on the railroad loading dock. Museum officials promptly acknowledged the safe arrival of the artworks, but how were they to explain about the wine to the sizable delegation from Orleans expected at the opening? Said *The Wichita Beacon*: "Local officials could hardly believe it could happen here – until it did." Time was short and local officials went to work and a special release was hustled through the state legislature. The bill was passed and moved on for the governor's signature while the exhibition was being hung in Wichita and the French were en route to the celebration, which was, indeed, observed according to Gallic tradition.

Wichita reciprocated by honoring the 550th birthday of a famous daughter of Orleans, Jeanne d'Arc. Orleans' young sister city sent on loan an exhibition of 50 art works by living American artists. A quarter of the works were by residents of Kansas. Sponsors who offered local support were Wichita's Bastian Foundation, Inc., the S.O. Beren Foundation, and Mid-Kansas Federal Savings and Loan Association. The opening in Orleans on December 13, 1979, was attended by Mr. and Mrs. Howard Wooden, who represented the City of Wichita and the museum.

Mrs. Navas' presence at the opening of the new museum building in 1977 was to be her final visit to Wichita. She died a year and a half later in New York. Memorial services were held in Wichita on April 3, 1979, at Plymouth Congregational Church. In 1980, Edgar Turner of Wichita was appointed by the district court to be his aunt's successor, serving as co-trustee of the Murdock Estate with Garner Shriver. ❧

Construction problems that allowed water to leak into the new museum building were recognized after it was occupied in 1977, but a systematic repair program did not start until late in 1979. During the next two years while repairs were in progress exhibitions and activities had to be curtailed. Yet volunteer activity during these years was energetic, significant acquisitions were made, attendance remained unexpectedly high, and a more-than-satisfactory exhibition schedule was maintained.

By late March 1981, most of the repairs had been completed. To celebrate, a special spring reception was presented by the Volunteer Alliance of the Friends of the Wichita Art Museum. Behind-the-scene tours were conducted for the public by staff members and museum volunteers. The response was enthusiastic and the effort generated a timely renewed interest in the museum.

The idea for a gallery of "art to touch" arose in the early 1980s from the the Volunteer Alliance in consultation with the education staff of the museum. In April 1980 a committee headed by Louise Beren sponsored the Vedere Ball to raise funds for the gallery. The guest of honor for the evening was the noted actor, writer, and art critic, Vincent Price. A banquet was held and the Duke Ellington Orchestra performed. The first art object for the Hands-On Gallery, a sculpture titled *Birdstone II* by the American artist Lawrence Beall Smith, was presented to the museum and dedicated to Mr. Price. Subsequently, 20 additional works including sculptures, textiles, and ceramics, were purchased.

The Museum's November 1980 *Newsletter* noted that "Only a few museums in the country can boast of such a gallery and we can be proud of this pioneer effort. . . . Children whether blind or sighted need to touch things in order to learn." The project's popularity soon called for enlarging the gallery and acquiring additional works so that changes in the exhibition could be made regularly. A second Vedere Ball was held in April 1982, again by a committee of Alliance volunteers and coordinated by Lynn Ruffin.

Another development during 1980 was the reorganization of the Mobile Gallery program. It was transformed into a Traveling Visual Arts Program financed largely by the Kansas Arts Commission. The project operated under a full-time curator who was responsible for circulating exhibitions to Kansas communities at minimal expense.

The five years beginning in 1980 were a time of outstanding exhibitions at the museum. One of the first, initially arranged by the Jewish Museum in New York City, was titled *Danzig 1939: Treasures of a Destroyed Community*. The unique exhibition was presented in large cities on the east and west coasts, with only one showing between, at Wichita. It comprised 135 ceremonial objects associated with communal life, private life, and worship in the Danzig community. All had been rescued and sent to the Jewish Theological Seminary in New York City just a month before the Nazi armies moved into Danzig in 1939 and destroyed the city.

A second important exhibition was a retrospective of paintings by one of America's most noted representational painters, Billy Morrow Jackson. Jackson was already known to Wichita, for he had been commissioned by the Volunteer Alliance to paint a large work as a special gift for the permanent collection. The painting, titled *Moments*, was completed shortly before the new museum opening in 1977 and is based upon his impressions of Wichita from a visit a year

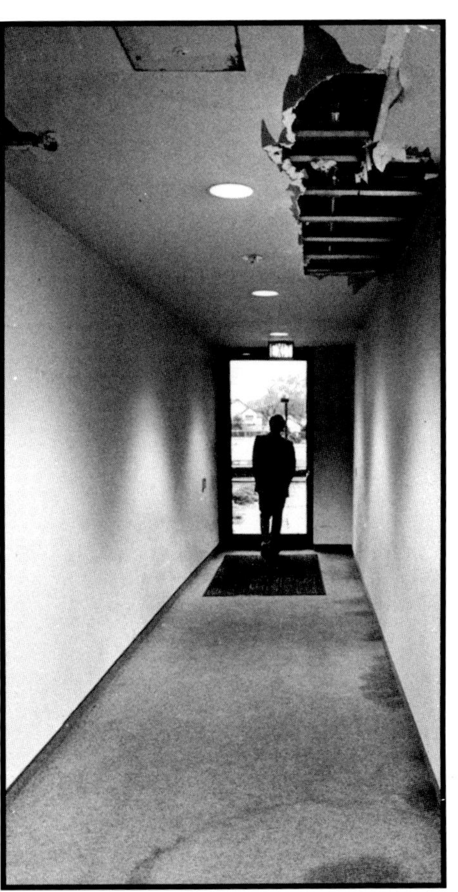

Activities at the museum had to be cut back while water leaks in the new building were repaired. The process took about two years beginning in 1979. Wichita Eagle photo

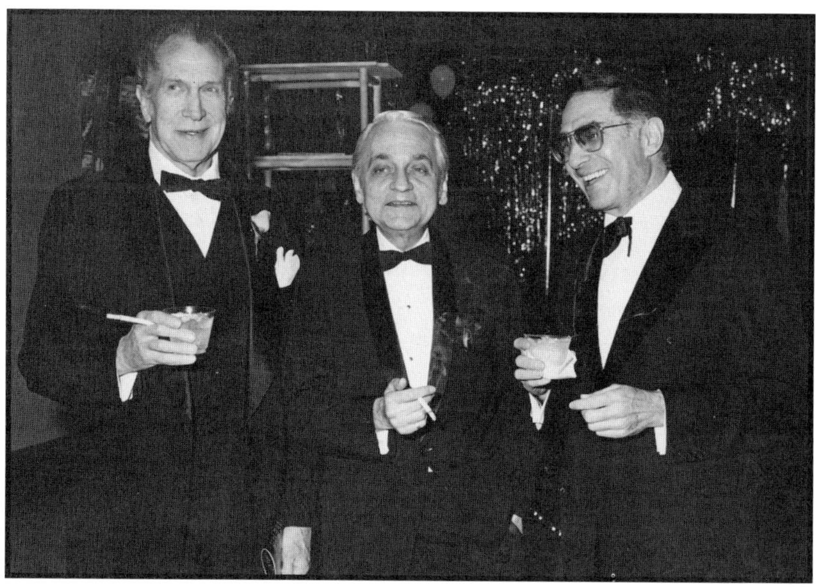

Vincent Price was the guest of honor at the 1980 Vedere Ball, a fund-raiser to establish a hands-on gallery. With Price are Howard Wooden, director of the museum, center, and S.O. "Bud" Beren.

The Hands-On Gallery features works of art to touch, not only for the blind and for children, but for museum visitors of all ages.

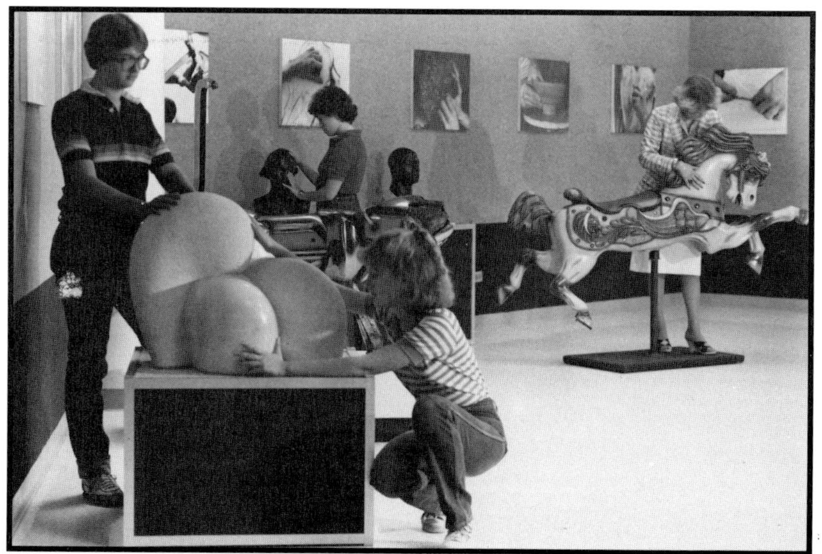

before he undertook the assignment.

Another major exhibition was presented in 1981 and titled *The Neglected Generation of American Realist Painters: 1930-1948.* The exhibition resulted from many years of research. It included realistic works painted by artists who had fallen into obscurity after World War II even though they had experienced considerable popularity during the Depression. The exhibition and its catalogue were prepared under a grant from the National Endowment for the Arts. It stimulated national interest in the art movements of the Depression period and particularly in the works of the realist painters.

It was also during this five-year period that the museum presented an exhibition in honor of David Bernard, now retired from the faculty of Wichita State University, where he taught for 35 years. The widely acclaimed printmaker and sculptor developed the university's respected printmaking program. The exhibition included 44 prints and four sculptures.

Museum Director Howard Wooden brought to fruition in this same period his long-time plan to offer a trilogy of exhibitions featuring the works of three noted artists with Kansas roots: painter John Noble, born in Wichita in 1874 when it was a cowtown in the heart of the Old West; Wichita native Bruce Moore, a sculptor; and Birger Sandzen, a Swedish immigrant who settled in Lindsborg, Kansas, and came to be recognized as a major American impressionist and post-impressionist during his long and prolific career. These three exhibitions, offered between 1982 and 1985, were organized and curated by Howard DaLee Spencer, the museum's curator of exhibitions and collections, with the financial assistance of Koch Industries. Scholarly catalogues accompanied each exhibition and were well received in the art literature of midwest American painting and sculpture. The Sandzen exhibit, the last of three, was presented in 1985 in celebration of the museum's 50th anniversary. ❧

CHAPTER NINE
1985

By proclamation of the mayor of Wichita, 1985 was named the "Year of the Wichita Art Museum" on January 8, 1985. Long before the proclamation was signed,

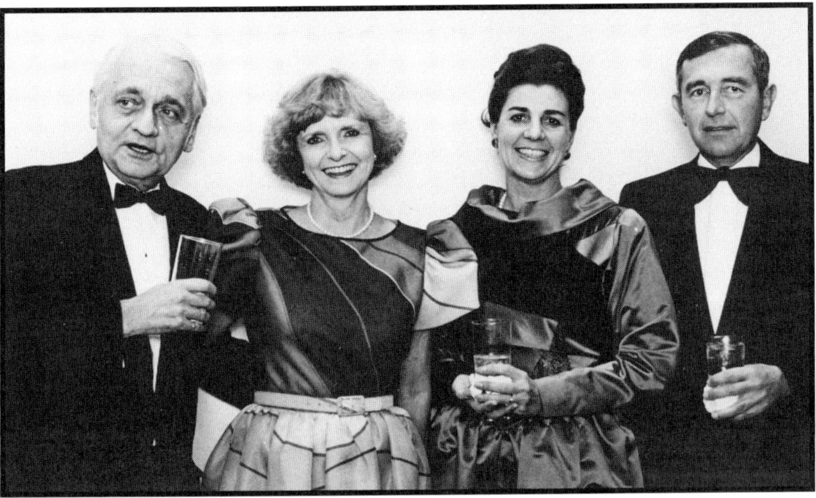

Celebrating at the 50th anniversary party for the museum are, left to right, Howard Wooden, museum director; Betty Minkler, chairman of the year-long celebration; Sarah Brasted, party chairman; and David Brasted. Wichita Eagle photo by C. Rollins

however, month-by-month plans for the museum's jubilee year were in place. Chairman Betty Minkler was joined by past presidents of WAMM and the Friends Volunteer Alliance to produce a varied calendar of celebrations including tours, receptions, dinners, a tea, a picnic, a variety show, a dance, and a fashion show.

The focal point of the jubilee year came on September 22, the date of the dedication of the first museum building 50 years earlier. The ceremonies included the unveiling of a gift from the Friends Volunteer Alliance, a handsome cor-ten steel sculpture titled *Watcher D* by noted New York artist Dorothy Dehner. The work was installed on the museum grounds east of the sculpture deck.

A birthday dinner and show on the evening of September 14 featured skits based on incidents at the museum, fireworks on the riverbank, and a grand finale of birthday cake and champagne.

The entire year was filled with activities. Just as when Gwendolyn Naftzger called for the support of museum volunteers in the 1960s, volunteers again came

forward to make 1985 a true jubilee.

Among the many commemorations was the museum gift shop's publication of a large-scale poster of the first painting purchased for the Murdock Collection, *Kansas Cornfield*, a work done in 1933 by the Kansas-born artist John Steuart Curry.

Many artworks were acquired during 1985. The first gift was the transfer on January 19 of Edward Henry Potthast's painting, *The Bathers.* It was donated from the John W. and Mildred L. Graves collection of 68 American impressionist paintings and prints, placed on permanent loan to the museum in 1984 and all destined as gifts to the museum through arrangements initiated by the owner, Mildred Graves Weir.

Many individuals and corporations honored the museum during the 50th-anniversary year. Sculptor Dorothy Dehner gave one of her works. Marguerite Rate of Halstead, Kansas, donated the Grant Wood suite of the four rare hand-colored lithographs, all executed in 1938 and titled *Fruits, Vegetables, Wild Flowers* and *Tame Flowers.* A surprise tribute came in the form of a colorful billboard placed by Donrey Outdoor Advertising featuring one of the museum's Charles M. Russell paintings of the Old West.

Early in 1985, Virginia and George Ablah established an acquisition fund for the development of the museum's British Watercolor Collection, which includes works by some of Britain's major watercolorists of the late 18th and 19th centuries.

The exhibition schedule through the jubilee year was extensive and diversified, including the third part of the Kansas trilogy, the Birger Sandzen retrospective. Several years earlier the museum had decided to provide an exhibition of Depression-era art during 1985, in part because interest in art of the period was growing and also because 1935, the year the museum was founded, was also the first year of the Federal Art Project under the Works Progress Administration. The museum presented an exhibition of 163 paintings, sculptures, prints, and drawings, some from the permanent collection and others on loan from museums, artists, and private collections. It was one of the most inclusive statements on the art of the Great Depression ever presented in an American museum. The catalogue is a detailed documentation of the creativity in art movements during the 1930s.

Mr. Wooden marked his 10th anniversary as director of the Wichita Art Museum during the summer of 1985, the lengthiest tenure of any director in the museum's history. Over the years he had become known for his scholarhip in art history and his polished lectures.[6]

As the jubilee year came to a close, the monumental contribution of time and energy by Betty Minkler, chairman for the year's events, and her husband Richard, was evident. Their labors, and those of many other volunteers and staff members, were the uncounted birthday gifts that assured an unforgettable 50th anniversary.

On November 20, 1985, a letter from the American Association of Museums announced that the Wichita Art Museum had met the association's standards for reaccreditation. First accredited in 1972, the museum in 1985 underwent a detailed survey of its operations, organization, and achievements, with special emphasis on collection management, by a representative of the AAM before being reaccredited, a fitting salute for the 50th anniversary. ❧

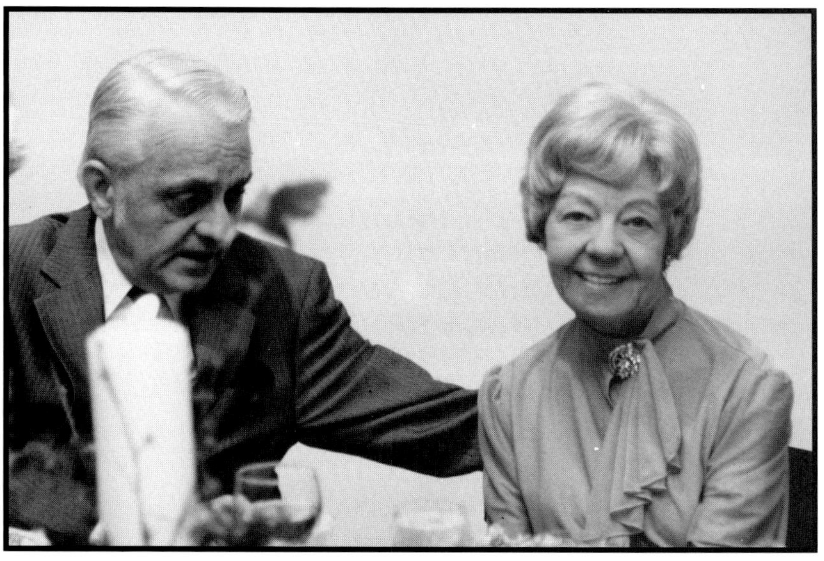

Mildred Graves Weir placed the John W. and Mildred L. Graves Collection of 68 paintings and prints on permanent loan to the museum in 1984.

In 1985 Virginia and George Ablah, shown here with museum director Howard Wooden, established an acquisition fund for the development of the museum's British Watercolor Collection.

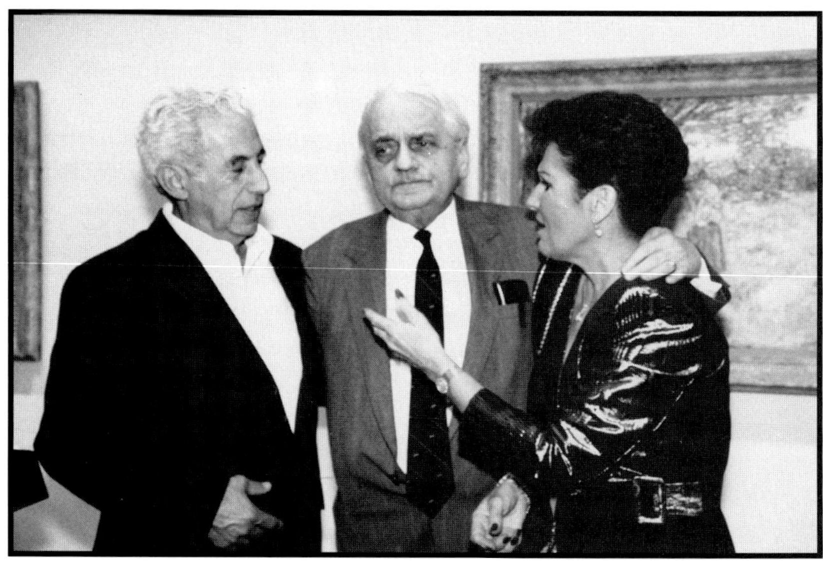

In 1986 the Junior League of Wichita, Inc., helped to start a storytelling tour for second-grade students. From its beginning as a "tiny box in the middle of the prairie," the museum had grown to the point that there was far too much for students to see in one trip. Even concentrating on a traveling exhibition or a special part of the permanent collections was sometimes too much for younger groups. The storytelling tours bring artists and art to life and elicit participation from the children. The docent-conducted tours are among the favorite school activities at the museum.

The museum's permanent collections were enhanced with the October 1986 acquisition of Douglas Abdell's monumental abstract sculpture, *Kaephae-Aekyad #2,* which was installed on the southwest campus next to the sculpture deck. In December 1986 two major works were acquired: *Ghost Women of Essaouira I* by Colleen Browning and *Champaign* by Billy Morrow Jackson.

In May 1987 the museum opened a major exhibition of avant-garde fiber works called *Fiber R/Evolution.* The installation of this exhibition resulted in the recognition of the museum's head preparator, Carole Branda. She received the Kansas Museum Association's Award of Excellence in recognition of her superior installation of traveling exhibitions.

This award followed on the heels of the achievements of Education Curator Novelene Ross, who earlier in the year received an Art Enhancer Award from the Kansas Association of Art Educators. As the museum moved into its second half century, it was clear that professional expertise and development of staff resources and talents were major concerns of the board and director.

Edgar Turner, a trustee of the Murdock estate, died in July 1987. Co-trustee Garner Shriver filed a petition in district court to appoint Roger Turner to take his place.

Recognition of the many years of support and service by several patrons of the Wichita Art Museum came at the end of 1987. Upper-level galleries were named in honor of Louise and S.O. Beren, Mildred Graves Weir, and Virginia and George Ablah. During this time the museum received its largest single gift in the form of a $1.18 million endowment trust from the Burneta Adair Estate. Mrs. Adair was a prominent Wichita philanthropist and long-time supporter of the Wichita Art Museum. Her will stipulated the use of the endowment for purchases of art and/or art research.

Staff and board members began reviewing the museum's collections and researching possible purchases. In 1990

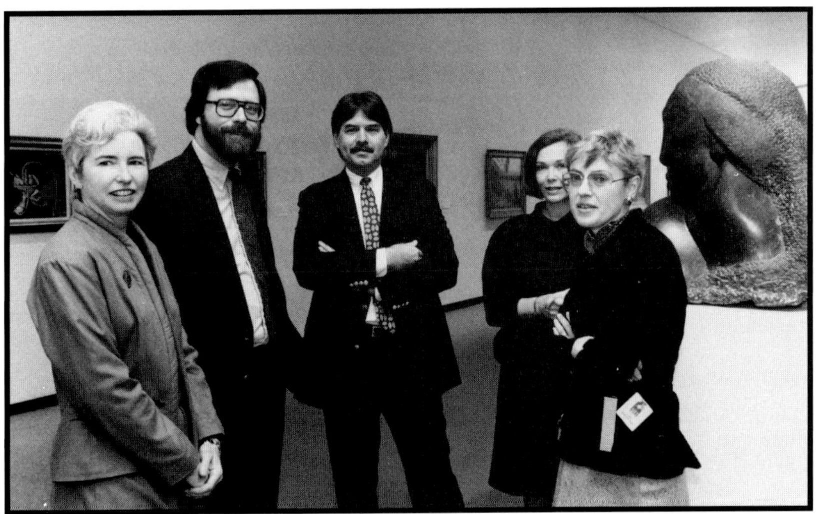

the first major purchase from the fund was made. *Printmakers of the Southwest* is a 46-piece collection from the estate of native Kansan Donald G. Humphrey, former director of the Philbrook Museum in Tulsa. This excellent collection includes work by 20th century artists such as John Sloan, R.C. Gorman, B.J.O. Nordfeldt, and Doel Reed. In announcing the acquisition, Georgia Stevens, president of the board, emphasized the effort to strengthen the museum's permanent collections. "This collection offers both an excellent survey of printmaking techniques and an extensive range of 20th century Southwest themes," she said.

Dr. J. Richard Gruber, center, became director of the museum in 1989. The management team in 1991 also included, left to right, Carol Zastoupil, curator of education; Douglas King, assistant director; Sharon White, director of development and public relations; and Dr. Novelene Ross, chief curator.

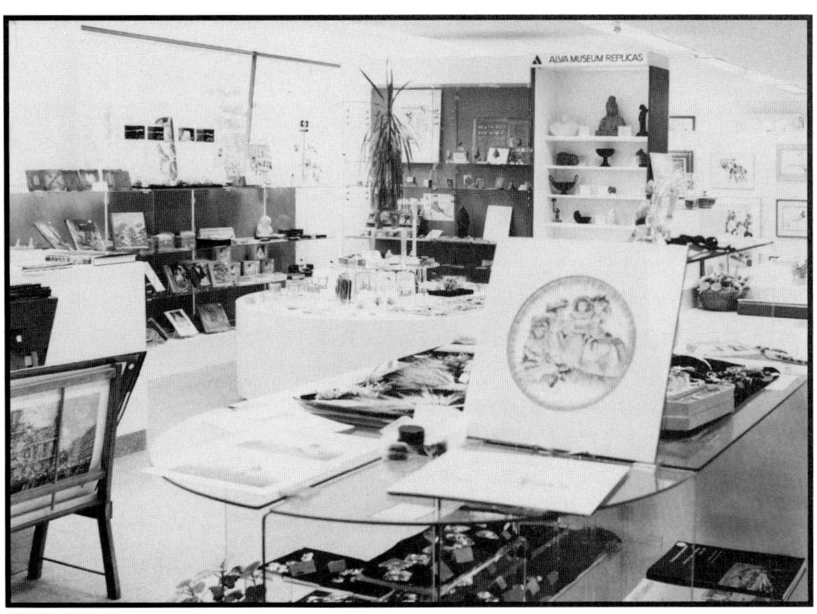

The museum shop and sales/rental gallery were combined under a full-time manager in 1989.

In July 1988 Howard Wooden, director of the museum since 1975, announced his plans to retire. Always a dedicated scholar, he wanted to devote more time to reading, writing, and speaking about art. A search committee was formed to find a replacement. At a reception for Mr. Wooden in November, it was announced that the auditorium was being renamed the Howard E. Wooden Lecture Hall. A book of 101 essays by Mr. Wooden on artworks collected by the museum since 1975 was published.

January 1989 heralded the arrival of Dr. J. Richard Gruber at the museum. He came to Wichita from the Memphis (Tennessee) Brooks Museum of Art. He completed a master's degree and doctorate in art history at the University of Kansas. Dr. Gruber's first lecture was on his doctoral subject, Thomas Hart Benton. His energy and enthusiasm helped renew the dedication of volunteers and staff to popular exhibits and programs to attract and educate a wide public audience.

One of the new director's first accomplishments was helping to organize the museums in Riverside. When L.W. Clapp urged the river area for a building site in the 1920s, and when museum officials decided to rebuild on the original site in the 1970s, they might not have known how increasingly important this area would be. It has become a cultural center of Wichita, home to three other museums in addition to the Wichita Art Museum. Old Cowtown Museum is a popular attraction showing Wichita as it was from 1865-1880. The Mid-America All-Indian Center opened along the banks of the Arkansas River in 1976, and the newest neighbor is Botanica, The Wichita Gardens, which opened to the public in 1987. The four museums joined to form Museums on the River, with joint marketing efforts, classes, and social events to increase the visibility of all the institutions. Together they have turned the eyes of downtown leaders, travel groups, and conventions to the Riverside area for entertainment and culture. The first cooperative programming was a four-week lecture series in July 1988. Colorful banners now line the streets in the area, and plans progress for further cooperative marketing.

During the first six months of 1989 museum operations were streamlined. This involved a reorganization of the board structure. The Wichita Art Museum Endowment Association and the Friends of the Wichita Art Museum were merged July 1 to create a new 20-member board to oversee the activities of the private side of the museum's operations. Together with the museum board appointed by the City Commission, they have the responsibility to run the museum, expand programs, provide funds, and plan activities.

Another merger involved the sales/rental gallery and the gift shop. Barbara Rensner, a long-time volunteer, accepted the full-time challenge of combining these two popular parts of the museum. The streamlined operations have resulted in greater net sales of artwork and gift items. Reorganization and restocking of the museum shop was completed in just six weeks in the summer of 1989. At the opening of the *Spirit of the American Southwest* exhibition on July 2, Mrs. Rensner had a new shop and much new merchandise. The shop specializes in representing local and regional artists, as well as being a source of art books and children's educational activities and games.

In 1989 the Christmas Committee of the Volunteer Alliance proposed changing *Christmas at the Art Museum* to *Holidays at the Wichita Art Museum*. The name change was accompanied by the addition of menorahs from the Jewish community and other holiday items and traditions from the Wichita area. The celebration was also expanded from two days to nine, and Christmas trees were displayed not only in the River Room, as in the past, but also throughout the museum. Attendance ran high throughout the nine days, confirming that the volunteers, headed by 1989 chairman Joan Schulz, were right in thinking that the museum had become an integral part of many people's holidays.

Karen Root and Susan Wilhite began managing the museum restaurant under contract in 1986. The restaurant, which can now seat 250 with the addition of seating in the River Room, has grown increasingly popular over the years. It began serving brunch on Sundays in 1989. Volunteers still assist in restaurant operations, and special events and luncheons are handled by a committee of the Volunteer Alliance.

With these popular changes and new programs, attendance at the museum increased more than 12 percent from 1988 to 1989. Acquisitions continued with an emphasis on American art, including works by John Steuart Curry, Thomas Hart Benton, Grace Hartigan, and Will Barnet. Twenty-eight small watercolors by Arthur Dove were presented to the museum by Bill Dove, the artist's son, in recognition of the foresight of Elizabeth Navas in purchasing three of Arthur Dove's early works.

Water leaks that had plagued the building since 1977 persisted. Various proposals, lawsuits, and stopgap measures had failed to solve the problem. Another attempt began in July 1989 when Architectural Wall Systems of Dallas, along with city maintenance personnel, began testing to find the cause of the leaks. In early 1990 the front entrance was closed to begin thorough waterproofing. In 1990 the city committed more than $600,000 to replace all the windows in the building.

Several major staff appointments were made in 1989 and 1990. Sharon White rejoined the Friends staff in late 1989 after a two-year absence. She returned as director of development and public relations. In January 1990, Dr. Novelene Ross was appointed chief curator after 17 years as education curator. Later that month Douglas King was appointed to the newly-created position of assistant director. With the appointment of Carol Zastoupil as curator of education in late 1990, the new manage-

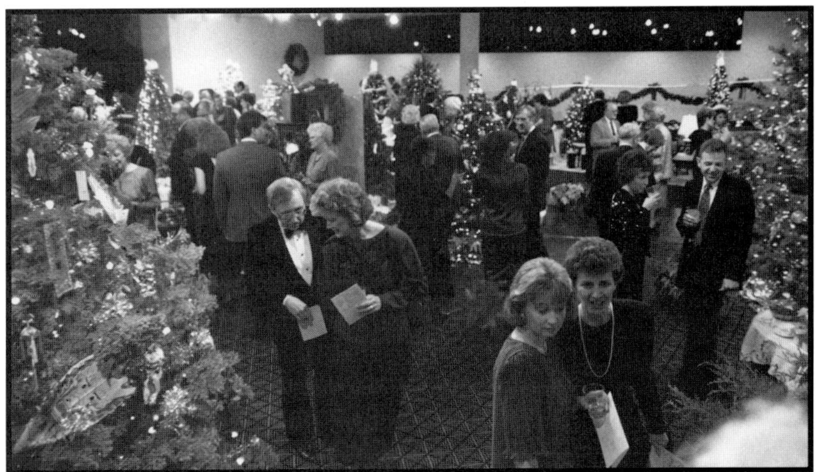

ment team was ready to work on exhibition plans, long-range goals, and increased visibility in the community.

During the 1990 celebration of the museum building's 55th anniversary, the galleries in the existing portions of the original building were painted in 1930s colors and reinstalled to exhibit some of the museum's key collections. The rotunda was hung with the Murdock portrait collection, and another gallery was devoted to 1930s Depression-era art.

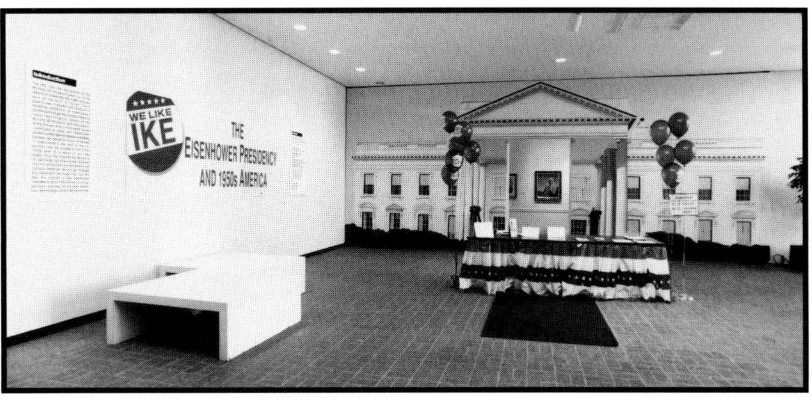

The museum's most ambitious exhibition ever was We Like Ike: The Eisenhower Presidency and 1950s America, *displayed in 1990 in conjunction with the 100th anniversary of the birth of Kansan Dwight Eisenhower.*

The first Murdock purchase, John Steuart Curry's *Kansas Cornfield*, has the place of honor there. Now as visitors enter the museum they immediately see the roots of the museum in the original galleries that hold the basis for all the Wichita Art Museum's collections.

In early 1990 the museum staff, board, and volunteers began planning for their most ambitious exhibition undertaking ever. In honor of the 100th anniversary of Dwight Eisenhower's birth, the museum, with the cooperation of the Eisenhower Center in Abilene, Kansas, began planning *We Like Ike: The Eisenhower Presidency and 1950s America*. One of the world's top museum installation designers, George Sexton, was brought in as a consultant. His plan called for the construction of 12 galleries within the exhibition space. Dondlinger Construction Company of Wichita was awarded the contract, and construction and installation of the exhibition of more than 500 objects was completed in less than three weeks.

In addition to the main exhibition galleries, companion exhibitions focused on art and functional design of the 1950s. Furniture, appliances, bicycles, toys, fads, American art movements, and such unexpected items as Tupperware appeared throughout the building to immerse visi-

tors in the time period. The museum restaurant featured a 1950s "blue plate special" daily, and volunteers, staff, visitors, and friends sported "We Like Ike" buttons and put "We Like Ike" campaign signs in their yards.

Friends of the Wichita Art Museum helped mount a series of events, lectures, and parties in conjunction with the exhibition. Events ranged from lectures by leading authorities on Eisenhower, the civil rights movement, and art of the 1950s, to a sock hop, a fashion show, and a one-woman play about Mamie Eisenhower. The exhibit was previewed at "Dinner With Ike," arranged by Sue Pryor on May 10. The public opening was Saturday, May 12.

The Wichita Art Museum began a new program in the fall of 1990 thanks to grants from the Kansas Arts Commission and Wichita Greyhound Charities. Karen Brady was hired as the museum's first part-time artist-in-residence. Students recommended by teachers in the public school system receive scholarship art classes. Ms. Brady also started a series of adult classes combining lecture and studio work and instituted public tours of the museum on Sunday afternoons.

A survey undertaken in 1989 reaffirmed the importance of the museum's permanent collection to the community. The board and staff began looking for ways to reach a wider segment of the community and set out to define the museum's purpose and goals. In September 1990, the board of directors adopted a statement that says in part that the museum's "purpose is to collect, preserve and exhibit American art, and educate the public about America's artistic heritage and evolving cultural identity." The statement says that the museum's collection policy "will expand areas of strength, particularly American art produced from 1900-1950, where the Wichita Art Museum already commands national prominence."

The work on long-range goals helped identify exhibition focuses, educational programs, and collection policies. In September 1990 the museum turned its attention westward in its first year-long exhibition series. Titled *Romance of the American West,* the year of September 1990-August 1991 was filled with exhibitions exploring native American art and culture, Old West and contemporary Western art, and focusing on pioneers in art, architecture, culture and technology.

Opening exhibitions for *Romance of the American West* were the nationally acclaimed *Native American Tradition: The American Indian Collection of the Lowe Art Museum* and *Sign Language: Contemporary Southwest Native America, Photographs by Skeet McAuley.* These exhibitions opened in September and proved to be the most popular exhibits ever with teachers and students. Docent-led tours were fully booked just two weeks after information went out. Many docents helped the children get in the spirit of the exhibits by dressing in western wear and donning Native American jewelry.

Other exhibitions on the western theme included *The Prairie Printmakers in the Southwest* and *Pikes Peak Vision: The Broadmoor Art Academy 1919-1945.* These were followed in the spring and summer of 1991 by *Masterpieces of the American West: Selections from the Anschutz Collection.* The collection of 81 paintings surveyed the painter's view of the West from the works of George Catlin and Alfred Jacob Miller through those of Georgia O'Keeffe and Jackson Pollock. At the beginning of the exhibition in April, the museum presented a two-day symposium on The Romance of the American West in Evolution, bringing together humanities scholars, museum professionals, and arts performers to explore the subjects so often portrayed and romanticized in art of the American West – the cowboy, the Indian, the frontier. The symposium was funded in part with a grant from the Kansas Committee for the Humanities. ❧

EPILOGUE

Louise Caldwell Murdock's bequest of an art collection for Wichita was a gift destined to call forth many more. It began as an idea in the mind of a person of vast generosity and foresight, its substance for a time no more than a piece of paper. The few who were aware of the idea and its portent were moved to assist her vision on its journey to reality. The path was neither short nor easy, but the goal became a magnetic force. By its 50th birthday, the museum Mrs. Murdock envisioned had undergone two external metamorphoses and a continuum of internal growth to emerge as a treasure house of gifts. These gifts express a universal urge for caring and sharing. They are symbols of the past for the present and for the future. ❧

1. It was widely thought that Louise Murdock's will describing her plan for an art collection intended it to honor her husband by stating "that it shall be named 'The Roland P. Murdock Collection.'" No distinction such as "Jr." or "Sr." was used, although her son was named in the same will as "my son, Roland P. Murdock." In the course of research for this book, it developed that opinion was not unanimous among surviving Murdock relatives and friends as to Louise Murdock's intentions. Some were sure she wanted to honor her husband, others strongly maintained she was naming their son, and a few felt confident she meant both. Further investigation confused the issue more when a delayed birth certificate was found at the Kansas Department of Vital Statistics dated June 26, 1922, stating that the son born to Roland P. and Louise Murdock on July 26, 1884, was named Roland Edwards Murdock. The earliest known record of the use of "Jr." with the son's name is on his grave marker in the the Murdock family plot in Highland Cemetery. Mrs. Navas would have been responsible for his funeral arrangements, including this inscription, for she faithfully carried out the instructions with which she was charged as executrix of the estate.

2. From the late 1920s until the dedication of the Wichita Art Museum on September 22, 1935, the planned structure was variously identified in the Wichita Park Board's minutes and elsewhere as the Art Building, the Art Institute, and the Art Institute Building.

3. Interesting comments may be found in the copy of Mrs. Navas' lecture of November 8, 1940, concerning the first 16 paintings that she had selected and sent to Wichita to begin the Murdock Collection. See the Appendix for excerpts.

4. The Wichita Art Museum's first board meeting, according to the only known copy of its minutes, took place on October 29, 1955, at 7:30 p.m. The original board members who could be reached at the time of this writing were unable to explain the disparity. The most logical conclusion appears to be that the minutes were in error in stating that the first meeting took place in October instead of November.

5. Architect Edward Barnes, when being shown the museum building for the first time, is recalled as having pronounced its rotunda a "little jewel." It was the generally expressed wish that this feature be retained in the 1963 and 1977 reconstructions.

6. A highlight of the jubilee year was the public lecture series given by Museum Director Wooden on four Sunday afternoons in March 1985. The topics were "Greece and Greek Cultural Heritage," "The Middle Ages: Looking Backward and Forward," "Renaissance: Revolution and Evolution in Art," and "Trends of the 19th and 20th Centuries in Art." A dinner was held after each lecture. The historical periods of the lectures were reflected in the menus and decorations. ❧

Appendix

Lecture by Elizabeth Navas, November 8, 1940, concerning the first 16 paintings selected for the Murdock Collection

The last world war was well started in its destructive terror, when Louise Caldwell Murdock in her own hand wrote in her last will and testament very simply and clearly her wishes for her townspeople. "All of my property held by my executors shall be put into a trust fund to be administered by them, and the interest accruing from this fund shall be used for the buying of an art collection for the City of Wichita providing a suitable place shall be provided for the housing of this collection and it shall be called the Roland P. Murdock Collection."

Perhaps the most important effect of these words has been the inspiration given to many people in Wichita in turning their thoughts to the various phases of Art; the founding of the Wichita Art Association is a noteworthy example.

The world is again in the midst of a terrible conflict and our people are thinking much of matters of defense. Forbes Watson has written, "we cannot limit ourselves to the physical problems of our defense. Vitality of the spirit calls for more. Let the barbarian force us to think only of powder and shell and already he will have won a terrible victory. A tremendous demand on our vitality is at hand. If we can meet the test, in vain will the defeatists whisper, 'what is the use' of painting, of sculpture, of poetry, of philosophy, of abstract thought, of faith, of delight, of happiness? If these have no use, what indeed are we defending? We are defending the liberty of the mind, the heart, our faith, the freedom to live a life in which we can sometimes use wings."

Should European centers of culture collapse, I, as an American, feel that our country must take the lead in carrying forward the activities of the mind and spirit – a challenge to individuals and communities.

As Lewis Mumford, art critic and philosopher has written: "The expressive arts have a particular message for us; for they have never abandoned the cultivation of the self; and they have done this by methods that are generally valid and not those which promote mental unbalance and corruption."

We are gathered here this evening for the installation of the initial group of paintings of the Roland P. Murdock Collection, founded by Louise Caldwell Murdock. The instructions of Mrs. Murdock were that American artists be given the preference in the forming of the collection. The sixteen artists included in this group are all American citizens. Nationality is not only a matter of birth and politics, in Art it is primarily a matter of environment. The artist is required only to keep faith with the American spirit for it is this alone which shall brand his art as American. The pictures have been hung in the southeast gallery, where they may be viewed later in the evening. At the moment, in talking about them, we are going to use the convenience of lantern slides.

(Mrs. Navas went on to describe the first 16 paintings she had selected. They were *Portrait of Billy Smith* by Thomas Eakins, *Hudson Sky* by John Sloan, *As Ships Go Sailing By* by Maurice Prendergast, *Mike McTeague* by George Luks, *Luxembourg Gardens* by Williams Glackens, *December Twilight* by Charles Burchfield, *Kansas Cornfield* by John Steuart Curry, *Sandwiches* by Reginald Marsh, *In Western Garb* by Henry Varnum Poor, *Beach Scene* by Guy Pene DuBois, *Portrait of the Painter's Wife* by Alexander James, *Promise Land, Long Island* by Louis Bouche, *Skyways* by Henry Mattson, *The Blue Chair* by George Grosz, *Hecate's Court* by Peggy Bacon, and *5 A.M.* by Edward Hopper.) ❧

Carol Hogan	October 1956 - June 1958
Richard Grove	October 1958 - February 1964
Sebastian Adler (Acting Director)	March 1964 - October 1964
Sebastian Adler	October 1964 - June 1966
John Petty, Curator	June 1966 - September 1967
Richard S. Teitz	September 1967 - August 1969
Jan von Adlmann	August 1969 - October 1972
J. Dennis Worley (Acting Administrative Director)	October 1972 - April 1973
George E. Vollmer (Acting Director)	April 1973 - August 1973
Sue M. Thurman	August 1973 - October 1973
George E. Vollmer (Acting Director)	October 1973 - March 1975
Howard E. Wooden	August 1975 - January 1989
J. Richard Gruber	January 1989 -

CHRONOLOGY

1915

April 20 — Louise Caldwell Murdock writes will providing for the purchase of an art collection for Wichita after the deaths of her heirs.

April 23 — Louise Caldwell Murdock's death. (Born 1858.)

April 27 — Will filed in probate court. Trustees: Elizabeth Stubblefield, John A. Parkinson.

Death of first of Murdock heirs, Rewey H. Caldwell (1832-1915), mother of Louise Murdock.

1917 — Elizabeth Stubblefield marries Rafael Navas; residence in New York City.

1920 — Wichita Art Association founded by Walter A. Vincent and C.A. Seward.

1921

January — Wichita Art Association chartered. Walter Vincent, first president.

1922 — Wichita Art Association opens art classes at Lassen Hotel Grill.

1925

June 9 — Resolution presented at meeting of the Board of Park Commissioners that the City of Wichita accept and qualify itself to receive the benefits of Louise Murdock's will, to construct necessary building, and provide for an issue of bonds by the city to pay costs. Motion carried.

June 17 — Wichita Art Association assigns committee of seven to promote building.

June 23 — Park Board President L.W. Clapp presents estimate of $75,000 for acquisition of grounds and construction of building(s) for museum. Request goes to City Commission to provide funds by bond issue.

July 6 — City Commissioners vote unanimously in favor of the bond issue and building an art museum.

1926

April 27 — L.W. Clapp authorized to negotiate with owners for tract of land on River Boulevard at South Sim Park Boulevard known as the Stackman farm.

May 11 — Clapp reaches agreement with owners of property and is authorized to execute a contract at price not to exceed $16,500 for 7.65 acres.

September 4 — Final arrangements made with the Stackman Building and Investment Corporation for purchase of land for $16,500.

1927

July 26 — L.W. Clapp makes trip east to investigate "art buildings."

1928

March 27   Park Board Commissioners authorize their president to execute agreement with Clarence S. Stein of New York as architect of the museum building.

1929

January 8   Architect Stein prepares large-scale drawing.

November 18   Building plans discussed at Park Board meeting, focusing on materials to be used.

1931

November 10   Resolution adopted declaring it necessary to proceed with construction of central portion of Wichita Art Institute Building, as it was then called.

1932

January 11   Park Commissioners make plans to visit site and pick location of building on the next day, January 12.

1934

July 23   Park Board appoints Godfrey Hartwell construction supervisor for a museum of 11,750 square feet, smaller than originally planned. Works Progress Administration workers will help dig footings.

September 24   City attorney draws up agreement between the Board of Park Commissioners and Wichita Art Association providing for maintenance and upkeep of Art Institute Building.

October 17   Clarence Stein asks approval of Park Board to appoint Lee Lowrie as sculptor to make models for ornaments of Art Institute Building. Approval granted.

1935

February 22   Death of second Murdock heir, Roland P. Murdock, Jr. (1884-1935).

March 11   Wichita Art Association agrees with Board of Park Commissioners to provide for maintenance and operation of Art Institute Building.

July 22   Members of the Board of Park Commissioners inspect the Art Institute Building prior to this date. Approving resolution passed.

September 22   Museum dedicated and opened to public.

1937

April 23   Death of Cornelia S. Caldwell (1861-1937), sister of Louise Murdock and last of heirs, activates trust for creation of the Roland P. Murdock Collection.

April 26   Resolution approved at Park Board meeting states that a building had been constructed in compliance with the Murdock will.

September 30   Order entered setting up perpetual trust under terms of Louise C. Murdock's will.

1938

May 29   Members of Allied Art Extension Courses present Bruce Moore's bronze sculpture, *St. Francis*, in memory of L.W. Clapp.

1939

June 7   First painting of the Murdock Collection, John Steuart Curry's *Kansas Cornfield*, hung in museum.

Death of Elizabeth Navas' husband, Rafael Navas.

1940

October 14   Henry J. Allen, Robert C. Foulston, Robert R. T. Aitchison meet to work out agreement for use of a portion of museum building for Murdock Collection. Mrs. Navas present for latter part of meeting.

November 8   Group of 16 paintings (including *Kansas Cornfield*) officially presented by trustees and accepted by city. Lecture by Mrs. Navas.

1942

November 23   Wichita Art Association reports it has purchased the late L. R. Hurd's residence, Third and Belmont, and has moved its headquarters there from the Wichita Art Museum.

1943

October 4   M.C. Naftzger, Florence Naftzger Evans, and Pauline Naftzger Lautz offer collection of prints in memory of parents, L.S. and Ida L. Naftzger. Accepted by Park Board.

October 19   M.C. Naftzger, Elizabeth Navas, Mrs. Charles Higginson, and Mrs. Walter Stippich propose formation of Advisory Council for Art Museum.

1945

September 19   Advisory Council created without legal status. Twelve members begin terms on October 1.

1949

January 19   Park Commissioners approve resolution increasing number of members of Advisory Council and establishing tenure of office and manner of appointment.

1951

September 10   Naftzger family offers 61 additions to their 1943 print collection gift. Accepted.

December 10   Joint resolution of City Commissioners, Park Board, and regents of University of Wichita transfers museum administration to the university under five-year experimental contract.

1953

December 2 — Park Board approves $10,000 for urgent repairs to museum.

1954

First Air Capital Annual Show held. (Later known as Kansas Artists' Annual and Kansas Artists' Biennial.)

February 11 — Reactivation and expansion of defunct Advisory Council proposed by President Harry Corbin, University of Wichita.

July 12 — Museum repairs under way.

1955

August 10 — Harry Corbin, president of University of Wichita, advises City Manager Eugene N. Smith that the university wishes to return management and operation of Wichita Art Museum to city at end of five-year agreement, December 31, 1956.

October 21 — Unexpected death of Eugene J. McFarland, University of Wichita Art Department head, results in a follow-up request from President Corbin for release from contract "as soon as possible."

November 1 — City Commission adopts special committee recommendation to create a Wichita Art Museum Board of Directors with administrative functions to assume direction at noon, December 1, 1955. Sam Bloomfield named first chairman of the board.

1956

October 1 — Carroll Edward Hogan, native of Iowa City, Iowa, assumes duties as first professional director of Wichita Art Museum.

October 8 — Death of John A. Parkinson, Murdock estate co-trustee.

1957

Judge E.E. Sattgast names Kansas Congressman Garner E. Shriver to replace the late John Parkinson.

Court assures city title to and control of Murdock Collection.

1958

June — Director Carroll Hogan resigns.

October 15 — Richard Grove assumes duties as museum's second director.

1959

May 9 & 14 — Wichita Art Museum and Wichita Art Association hold joint meetings at Lassen Hotel and association's Belmont headquarters to explore merging.

November 23 — New volunteer organization adopts name Wichita Art Museum Members with the acronym WAMM. Application made for corporate status.

1960

March 9   Corporate status achieved for WAMM.

October 10   Air conditioning and new vault included in $300,000 capital improvement bond program approved by Park Board.

1962

April 6   Kansas Supreme Court returns Caldwell-Murdock Building, source of Murdock trust income, to tax rolls, effectively ending growth of Murdock Collection.

August 21   City Commission approves $150,000 for addition of museum building wings totaling 10,087 square feet. Snodgrass & Sons Construction Co. successful bidder.

September   Representatives of Wichita Art Museum and Wichita Art Association meet four times to further examine merger. Additional meetings held on October 23 and December 8.

November 7   Firm of Schaefer, Schirmer and Eflin employed for wings and other improvements.

1963

January 2   Sebastian J. Adler, Jr., comes from Sioux Falls, South Dakota, to be Richard Grove's assistant, a newly-created position.

March 25   Ground breaking for museum wings addition.

April 1-7   First citywide museum membership drive.

1964

January 16   Richard Grove resigns as museum director. Assistant Sebastian Adler appointed acting director.

March 19   Wichita Art Museum Members' 1950 Articles of Incorporation amended to change corporate name to The Wichita Art Museum Members Foundation.

July 16   Sale of Caldwell-Murdock building for $110,000.

November   Sebastian Adler named director.

November 16   First curator, Jon Nelson from University of Minnesota Art Gallery, hired.

1965

October 21   Director Adler fired, followed by resignations of five Wichita Art Museum Board members. Adler reinstated after interim appointment as "Protector of Art."

| December 16 | Proposed set of by-laws presented to Wichita Art Museum Board. |

1966

January	Federal grant of $33,515 over three years obtained for implementing a Mobile Gallery Van program for rural Kansas schools.
June 10	Following May resignation of Curator Jon Nelson, John Petty from University of Arizona Art Gallery, Tucson, becomes new curator.
July 1	Director Adler accepts position as director of Contemporary Arts Association, Houston, Texas. Curator John Petty becomes acting director.
November 14	Mobile Gallery Van dedicated in public ceremony downtown.

1967

| September 15 | Richard Stuart Teitz becomes Wichita Art Museum's fourth director. |

1968

February 15	William B. Stevens, Jr., from Rhode Island School of Design, appointed Wichita Art Museum curator following 1967 resignation of Curator John Petty.
	Faye Chambers Davison gives gift collection of 26 paintings by Edmund L. Davison and colleagues.
July 1	Mary Lee Archer becomes WAMM secretary.

1969

January 28	City Commission authorizes feasibility study for new museum.
March 17	Ford Foundation grant of $12,500 obtained for printing catalogue of Murdock Collection.
June 1	William Stevens, curator, resigns to become director of Pennsylvania Academy of Fine Arts in Philadelphia.
September 1	Richard Teitz resigns to return to Worcester (Massachusetts) Art Museum as assistant director. Jan Ernst von Adlmann comes from Tampa Bay Art Center in Florida to be new Wichita Art Museum director. Von Adlmann's curator was George Tomko. He also appointed the first curator of education, Sue Hennum.
October 3 - November 1	*Kitsch, the Grotesque Around Us,* exhibition originated at Wichita Art Museum.

1970

| December | Wichita Art Museum Board resolves to notify City Commission of its displeasure with City Manager Ralph Wulz's plan to reorganize city boards. The vote is 5-1 with one abstention. |

1972

January   First meeting of "The Young at 'Art," Max Schaible, president.

February 28   Wichita Art Museum accreditation by American Association of Museums announced by Director von Adlmann.

December 1   Director von Adlmann resigns to go to Long Beach (California) Museum of Art. J. Dennis Worley becomes interim acting director.

1973

March 27   Board accepts three staff resignations: J. Dennis Worley, acting director; J. Daniel Selig, curator; and Barry Jordan, director of finance.

City Commission allocates $3.5 million for new museum building.

April 15   George Vollmer named acting director on this date when Worley's resignation becomes effective. He appoints Curator Pamela Kingsbury and Curator of Education Novelene Ross.

August to October   Sue McWhirter Thurman arrives as new director from chairmanship of Rutgers University's Douglas College Department of Art. Illness soon necessitates her resignation. George Vollmer again fills the gap.

Prolonged consideration given by museum board to six potential sites for new building.

August 14   Presentation of Charles M. Russell Collection in memory of M.C. Naftzger.

1974

March   Three museum consultants -- Dr. Richard McLanathan, George Seybolt, and Kyran McGrath — meet with board about museum sites.

June 1   Mary Lee Archer becomes administrative secretary to the director.

August 28   Decision reached to build new museum at original location on Stackman Drive.

December 11   The architectural firm of Edward Larrabee Barnes, New York, selected to execute design for expansion and remodeling of museum. Wichita's Platt-Adams-Braht & Associates to head planning, execution, management.

1975

June 25   Wichita Art Museum's resolution to expand its board from 10 to 12 members fails in tie vote of City Commission.

August   Howard E. Wooden comes from directorship of Sheldon Swope Art Gallery in Terre Haute, Indiana, to become director of Wichita Art Museum.

December 29   The Law Company of Wichita awarded Wichita Art Museum construction contract, totalling $2.7 million.

1976

January 5-10 — Museum moves to temporary quarters, Litwin Building, 200 East Douglas. Reopens January 27.

January 10 — "Farewell to Old Museum" benefit.

October 3 — Membership drive starts with "Hard Hat" party. (Goal is 2,000 members from existing 750).

Meeting of Wichita Art Museum Members Foundation called to change name to "Friends of the Wichita Art Museum" and for general reorganization of boards.

1977

August — The Victor Murdock Trust approves establishment of two-year lecture series, "The Victor Murdock Lectures on Art," beginning fall of 1977.

October 23 — Public reopening of museum with dedication ceremonies and celebrations. Exhibition: *5,000 Years of Art*, loan from Metropolitan Museum of Art.

October — *Art Gallery* magazine features extensive coverage of city and museum.

November — Structural problems become apparent in new building. Repeated repair efforts ineffective. City files lawsuit. Litigation ends in 1983 with out-of-court settlement.

1978

May 14-June 14 — *Artists of Orleans* exhibition on loan from France.

October 4-31 — First "Very Special Arts Festival," a non-competitive show for the disabled.

October 7 — Sculpture deck dedication. *Vertebrae Number 11* by Henry Moore presented in the name of Frank and Dan Carney by Friends and Franchisees of Pizza Hut Companies.

Museum's first birthday party celebration in new building.

1979

March 30 — Death of Mrs. Navas in New York City.

June 29 — Entire Murdock Collection (167 pieces), collected 1939 to 1962, on dispaly as a tribute to Mrs. Navas.

November — Wichita assembles exhibition of recent American art for people of Orleans, France, to celebrate 550th birthday of Jeanne d'Arc.

1980

February 17 -
March 16   *Wichita Salutes Orleans* exhibition returned for showing in Wichita.

Edgar Turner named Murdock estate trustee, replacing his aunt, Mrs. Navas.

April 2   First Vedere Ball, benefit for Hands-On Gallery.

September   Traveling Visual Arts Program developed to replace Mobile Gallery Van.

November 6   Hands-On Gallery opening.

December 20   Mary Lee Archer becomes Executive Assistant, a newly-created position.

1982

April 17   Second Vedere Ball benefit for Hands-On Gallery.

October 24 -
November 28   *John Noble Retrospective.*

December 2   Elizabeth Galland bequest, Birge Harrison's *The Old Sawmill*, purchased as addition to Murdock Collection.

1984

September 16 -
October 14   *Bruce Moore Retrospective,* joint exhibitions at Wichita Art Museum and Wichita Art Association sponsored by Koch Industries.

December 1 -
February 3   Exhibition of John and Mildred Graves Collection of American Impressionists, received on permanent loan from Mildred Graves Weir.

1985

January 8   Proclamation by Wichita City Commission of 1985 as the "Year of the Wichita Art Museum."

September 14   50th anniversary birthday party.

September 22   50th anniversary public reception marking date of Art Museum's dedication in 1935. Unveiling of Dorothy Dehner's *Watcher D.*

November 9   "Depression Dinner" celebrates 50th anniversary of founding of the Wichita Art Museum and federal Works Progress Administration.

November 20   Wichita Art Museum reaccredited by the American Association of Museums.

1986

May	Junior League of Wichita, Inc. awards $6,700 to Wichita Art Museum to inaugurate storytelling tour for second grade students.
July 25	The art museum van, transporting art works from New York to Wichita, involved in traffic accident, causing major damage to the van and several works of art.
July-August	Museum begins a four-week film series on Sunday afternoons.
October	Douglas Abdell's monumental abstract sculpture, *Kaephae-Aekyad #2* installed on southwest museum campus adjacent to sculputre deck.
December	Two major works of art acquired: *Ghost Women of Essaouira I* by Colleen Browning and *Champaign* by Billy Morrow Jackson.

1987

April	Education Curator Novelene Ross receives Art Enhance Award from Kansas Association of Art Educators.
May 1	New art van is delivered to the musuem.
May 1	Museum opens major exhibition of avant-garde fiber works organized by Milwaukee Art Museum and the University Art Museum at the University of Wisconsin-Milwaukee. Preparator Carole Branda later receives 1987 Award of Excellence from the Kansas Museum Association in recognition of her superior installation of traveling exhibitions, including this show.
July 5	Murdock Trustee Edgar Turner dies.
October 24	Large upper-level gallery dedicated to Louise and S.O. Beren in recognition of their long-term support and service.
December 4	Major upper-level gallery dedicated to Mildred Graves Weir. Upper-level reception gallery dedicated to Virginia and George Ablah.
December 4-6	Sunday afternoon attendance at *Christmas at the Art Museum* produces the largest number of guests since opening of the new museum in 1977.
December	The Wichita Art Museum receives largest endowment to date, $1.18 million, from the Burneta Adair Estate for art purchases and/or art research.

1988

February	Roger Turner is appointed co-trustee of Murdock Estate, succeeding Edgar Turner.
May 7	Delegation from Wichita's sister city, Haiphong, China, visits the museum.

May 31	The Alice Hook estate sale opens, with proceeds designated to be used for the purchase of an artwork as a memorial to Enos Hook.
July	Director Howard Wooden announces retirement plans; search begins for new museum director.
November - December	The auditorium's name is changed to the Howard E. Wooden Lecture Hall. Director Wooden's book of 101 essays on acquisitions for the permanent collection since 1975 is published.

1989

January 17	J. Richard Gruber assumes duties as director of the Wichita Art Museum.
March	Meetings among Wichita Art Museum, Old Cowtown Museum, Mid-American All-Indian Center Museum, and Botanica result in formation of "Museums on the River." Joint educational and marketing programs are planned.
March	Wichita Art Museum Endowment Association merged with Friends of the Wichita Art Museum. A new 20- member board assumes duties July 1.
April	Director Gruber presents lecture series on Thomas Hart Benton.
June	Final preparations are made for major summer exhibition *The Spirit of the American Southwest*, curated by Dr. Gruber and Dr. Novelene Ross, Curator of Education.
July 5	Museum restaurant opens for Saturday lunch and Sunday brunch.
July 19	Barbara Rensner becomes first full-time paid manager of the Museum Shop. Shop is merged with former Sales/Rental Gallery.
July 17	Architectural Wall Systems of Dallas and city maintenance personnel begin testing museum building to find cause of persistent water leaks.
November	Sharon White named Director of Development and Public Relations.
December	Traditional *Holidays at the Art Museum* celebration extended from two days to nine.
December	Attendance for 1989 increases more than 12 percent from 1988.

1990

January	Dr. Novelene Ross appointed Chief Curator of the museum after serving as Education Curator for 17 years.
January 30	Douglas King is appointed to newly-created position of Assistant Director.

<table>
<tr><td>February</td><td>Galleries and hallway of existing portion of the original museum building are painted and reinstalled with permanent collection to celebrate 55th anniversary of the museum.</td></tr>
<tr><td>May 12-
August 26</td><td>*We Like Ike: The Eisenhower Presidency and 1950s America* exhibition.</td></tr>
<tr><td>September</td><td>Year-long series of exhibitions on the *Romance of the American West* begins.</td></tr>
<tr><td>December</td><td>Carol Zastoupil is appointed Education Curator.</td></tr>
</table>

1991

<table>
<tr><td>April 14-
August 11</td><td>*Masterpieces of the American West: Selections from the Anschutz Collection* on display.</td></tr>
<tr><td>April 19-20</td><td>Symposium on *The Romance of the American West in Evolution.*</td></tr>
</table>